First Impressions

Chet Kostrzewa

Copyright © 2024 Chet Kostrzewa
All rights reserved.
ISBN: 979-8-3303-2456-9

DEDICATION

Despite what Chuck Noland and Wilson may have thought, it does take a team. Thank you always, Susan and Kyle

ACKNOWLEDGMENTS

Digital technology has made the process of making and distributing high quality images reasonably accessible to everyone. As always, however, there remains a wide chasm between launching a snapshot onto social media and producing what might be considered a professional image. A big step in bridging that gap comes from finding your photographic voice. A short list of professional photographers I find particularly helpful in forging my own path includes (but is not limited to) the following:

James Popsys; Andrew Banner; Mark Denny; Nigel Danson; and Simon D'Entremont

All these true professionals are endlessly inspirational and educational and are readily followed through their websites and UTube channels. I highly recommend spending some considerable time learning from them.

You never get a second chance to make a first impression.

Will Rogers

After years in Southern California, a five-year relocation to the desert has quickly rolled by, with hardly a glance in the rear-view mirror. On impulse, I recently joined the horde of summer visitors converging on the California coast for a short 'disneyland' break.

Decades earlier I lived for a period in Europe. The experience was profoundly educational, transformational and occasionally jarring. Most notable was the revelation of how significantly the European mental vision of America differed from our own self beliefs and conceits.

Walking the beach streets of Santa Monica, I found my five-year absence made it look both familiar and unsettling at the same time. I realized this was a perfect opportunity to imagine and photograph new first impressions.

We might all be well advised to reflect on what first impressions visitors from any location take home with them, as we grapple to find a path forward in these challenging times.

Tucson, Arizona
July 2024

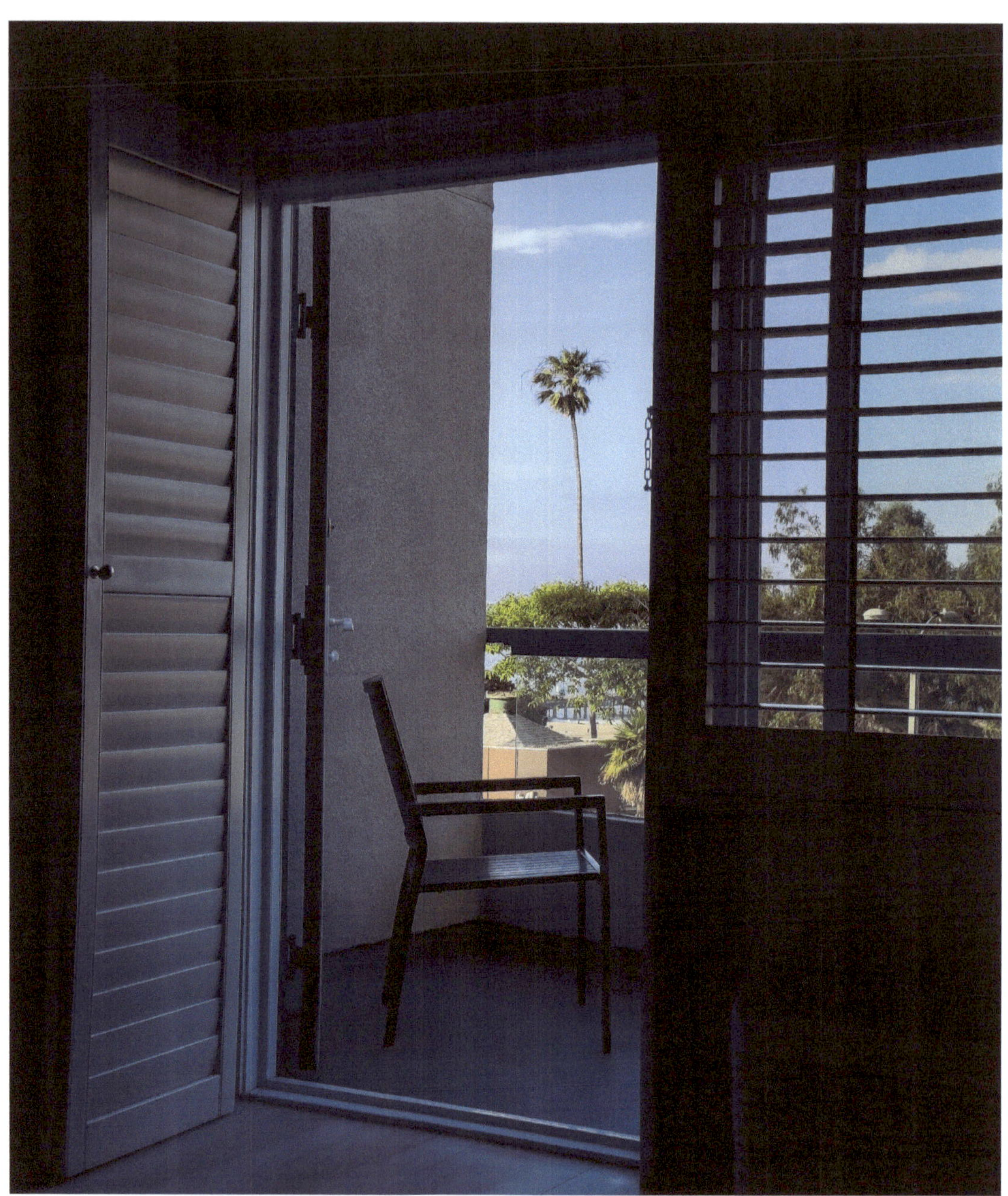

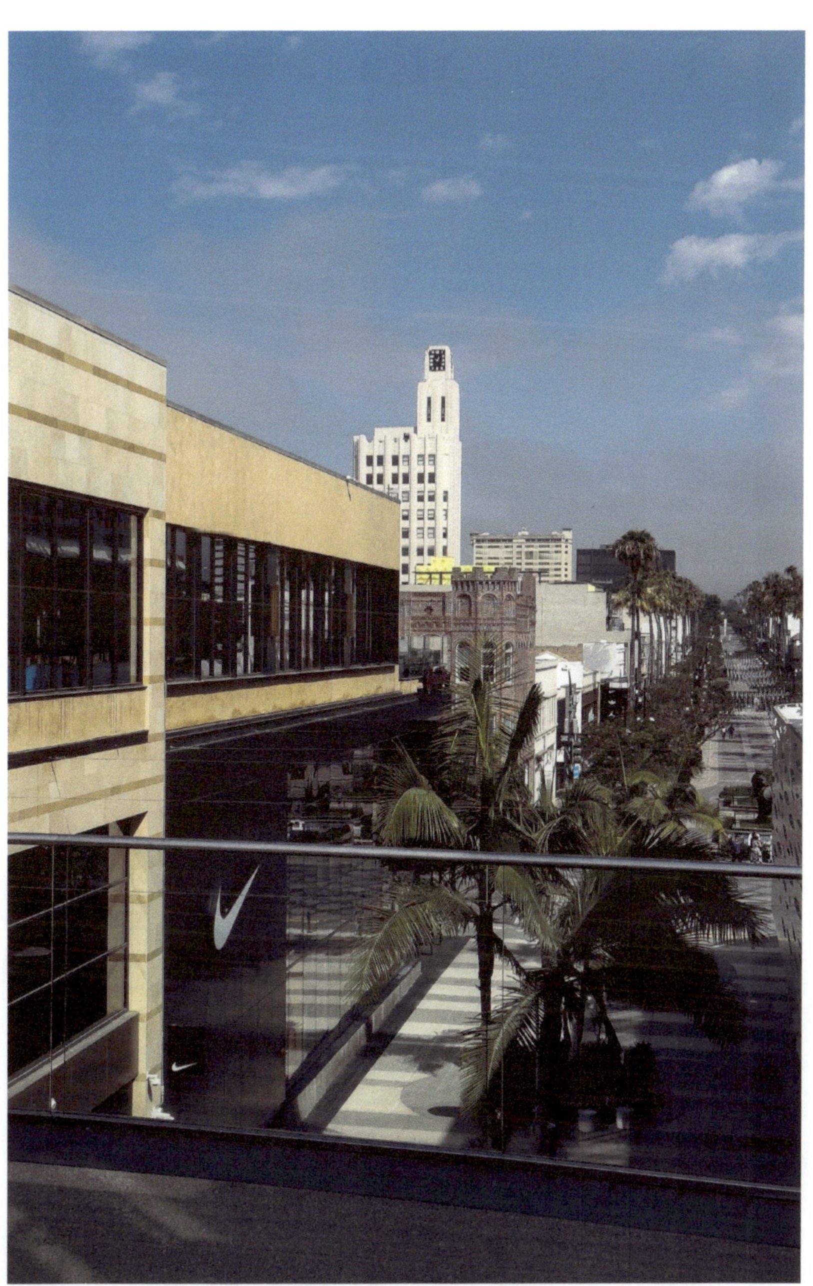

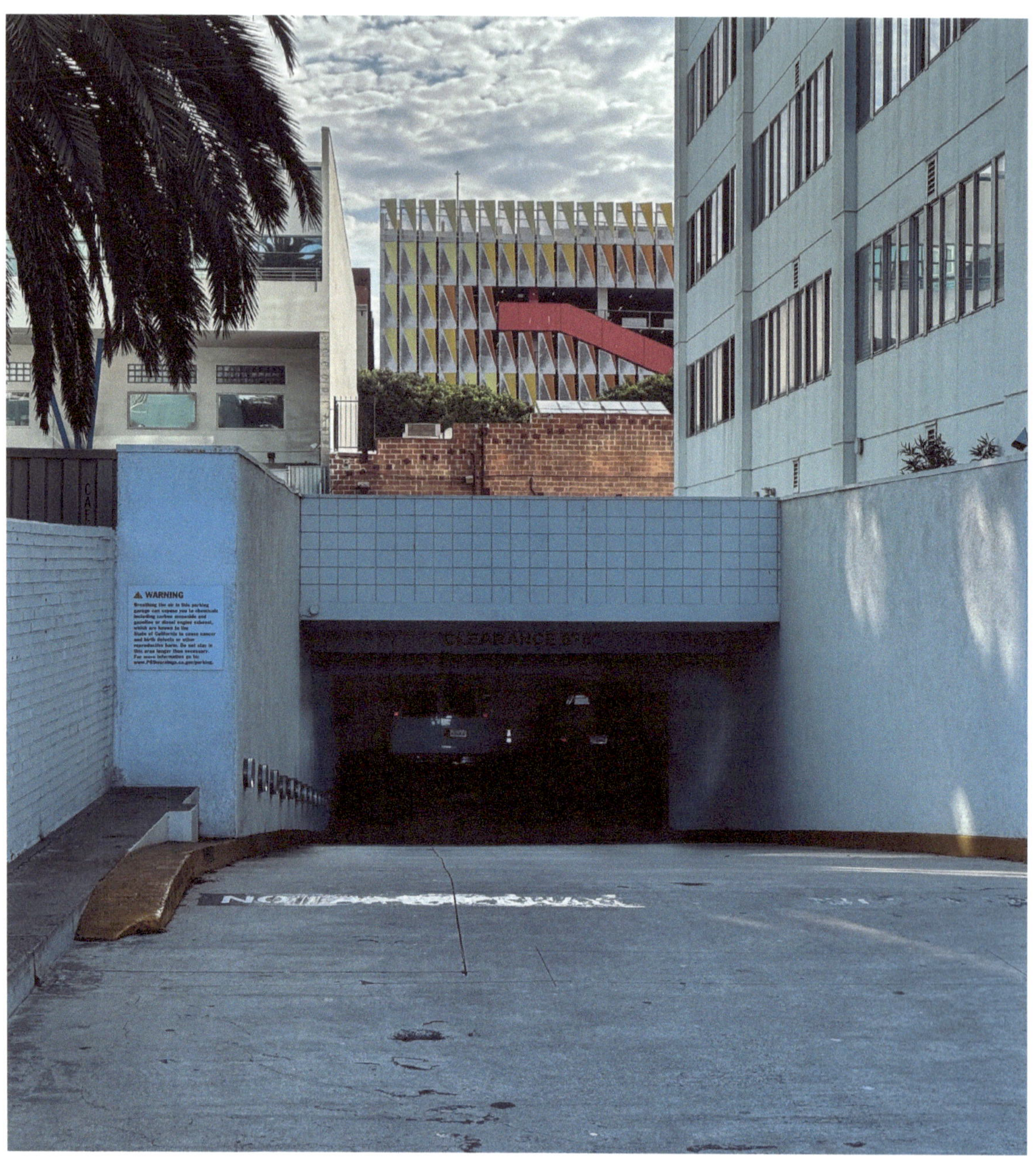
⚠ WARNING
Breathing the air in this parking
garage can expose you to chemicals
including carbon monoxide and
gasoline or diesel engine exhaust,
which are known to the
State of California to cause cancer
and birth defects or other
reproductive harm. Do not stay in
this area longer than necessary.
For more information go to:
www.P65warnings.ca.gov/parking.

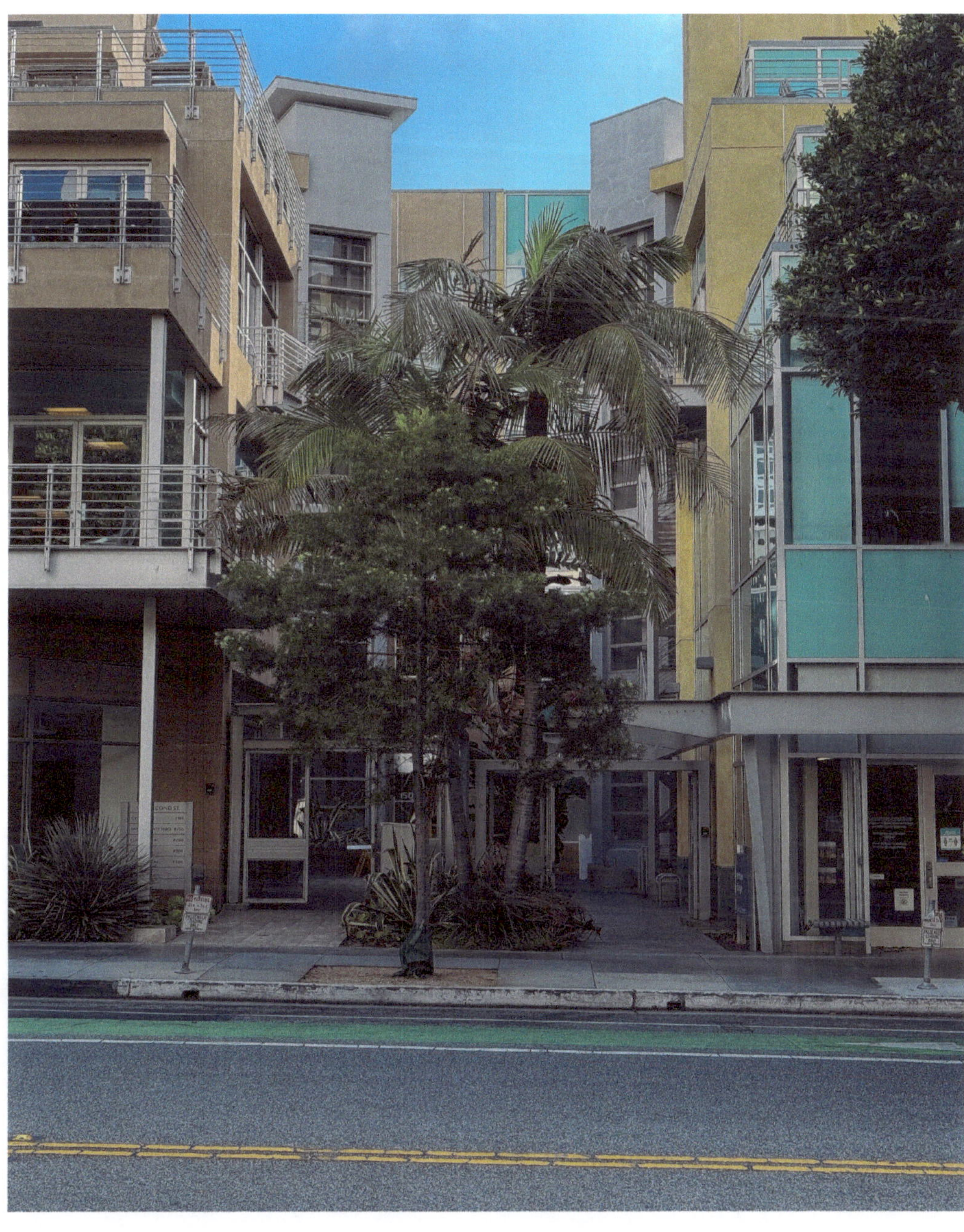

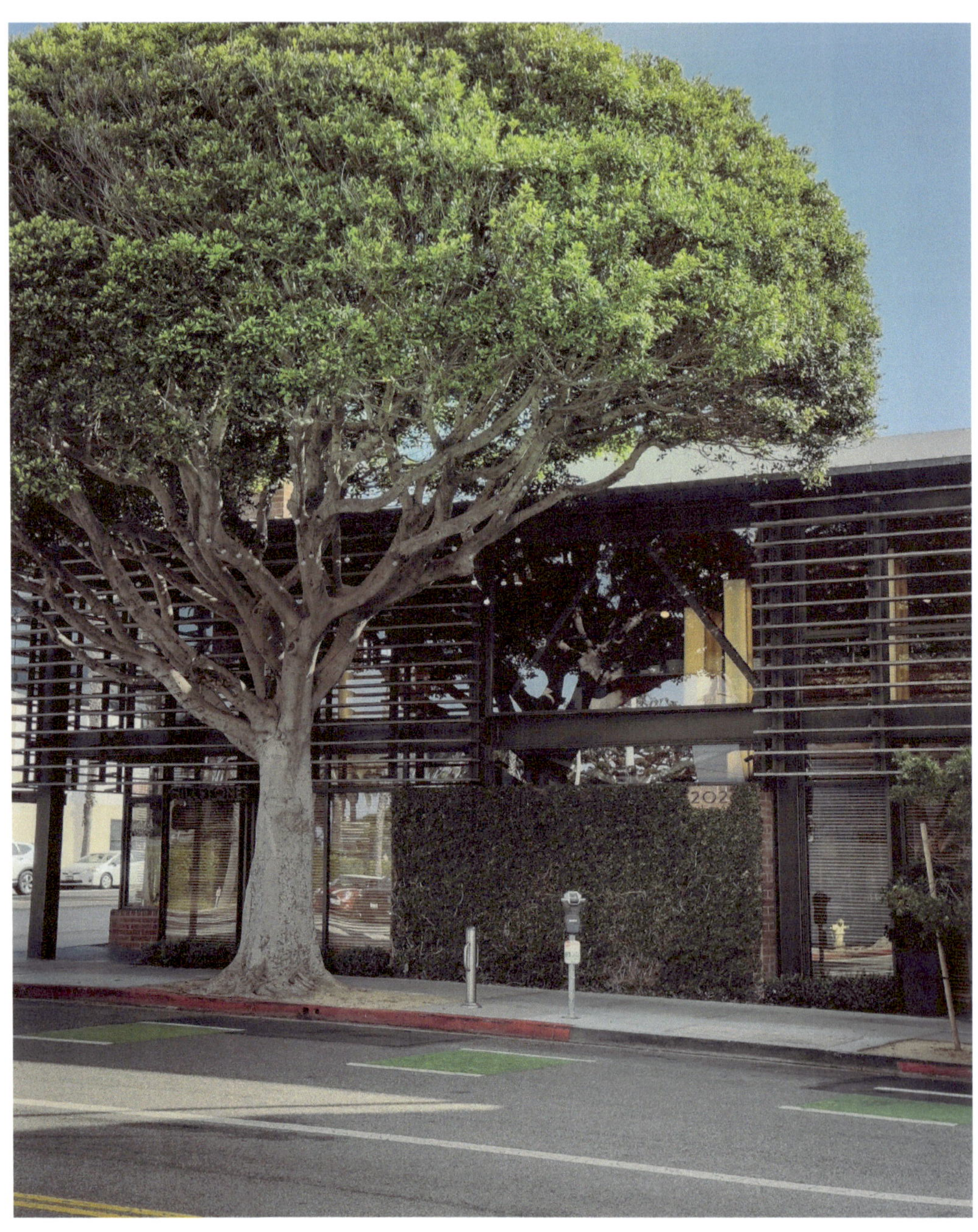

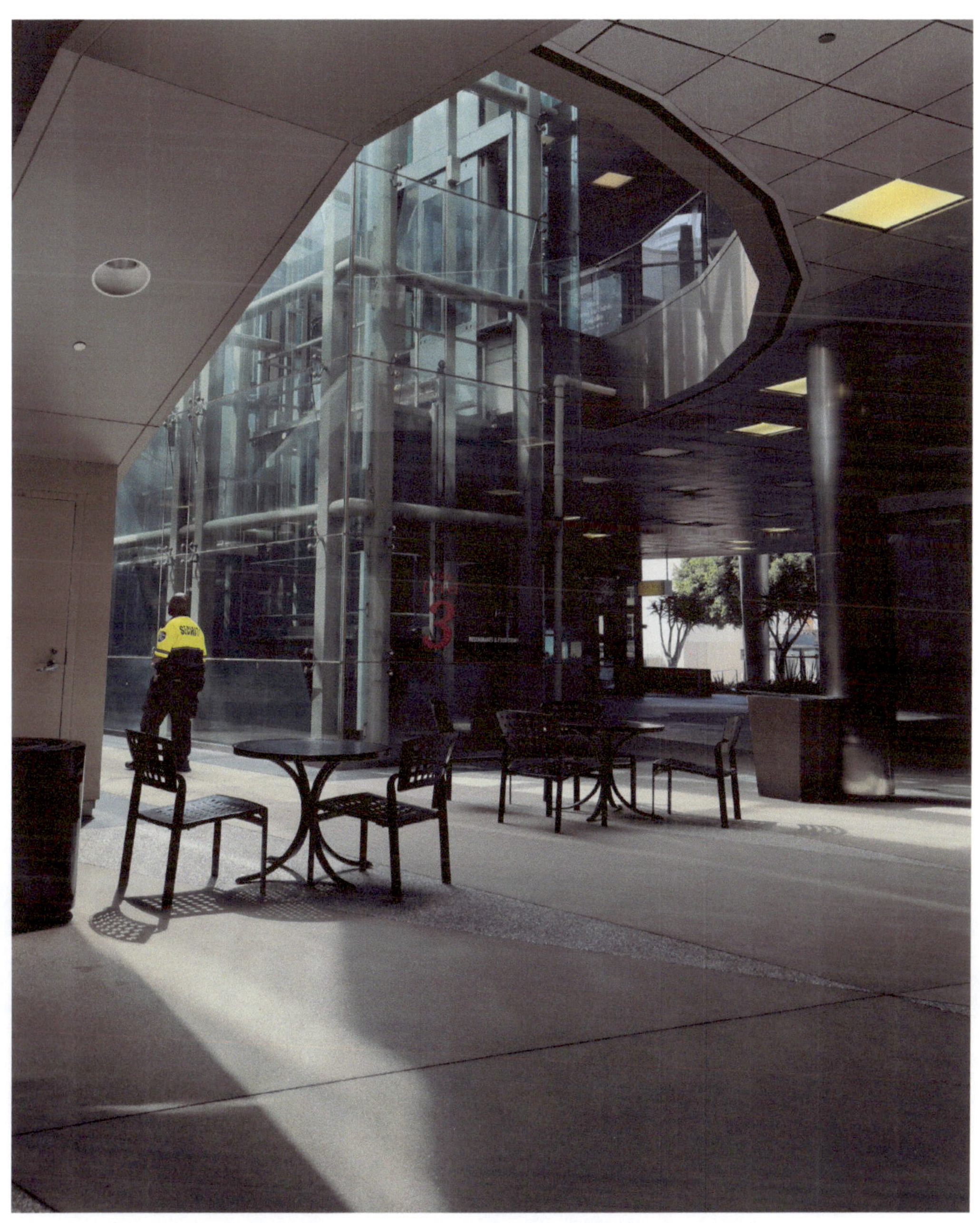

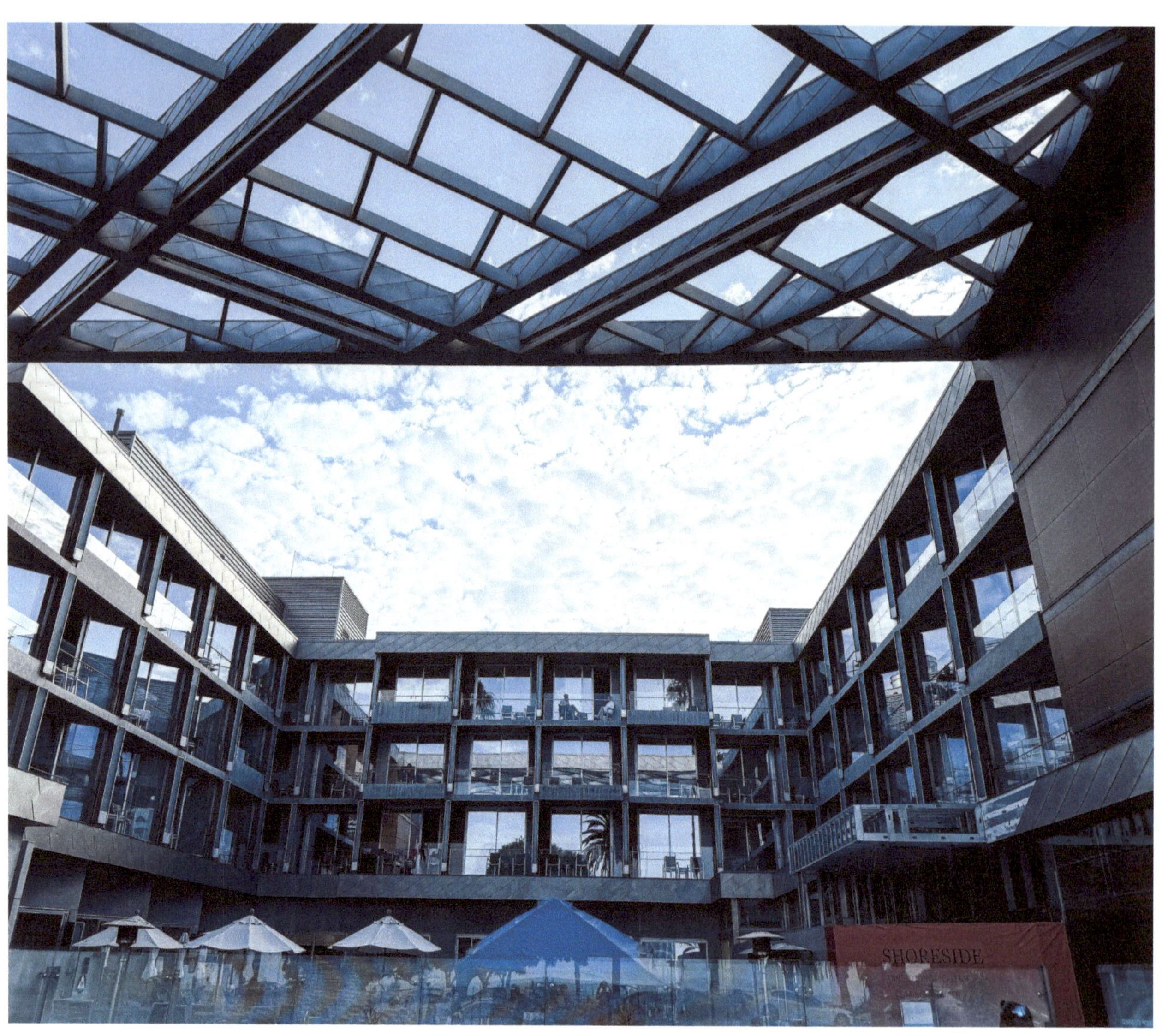

SHORESIDE

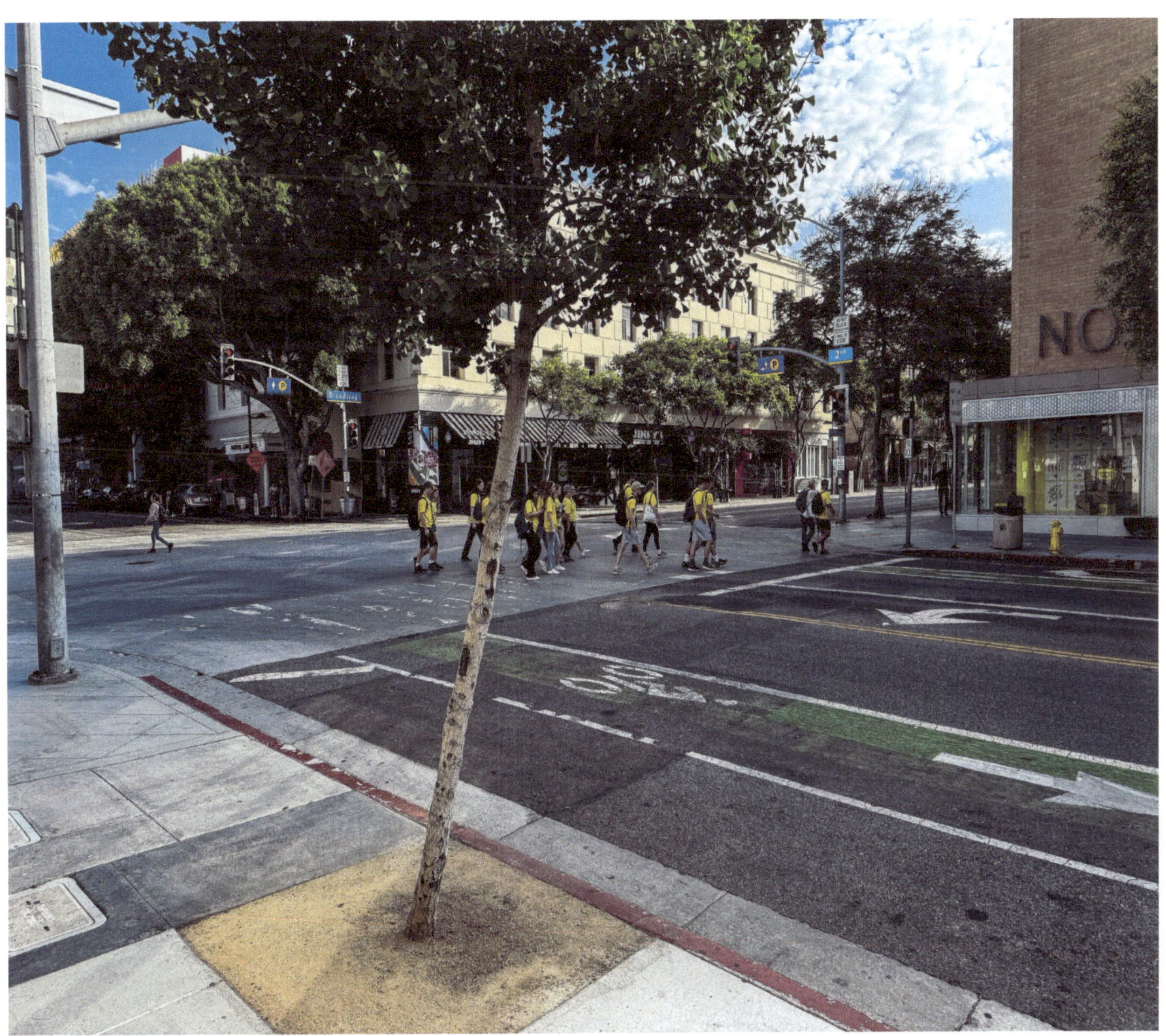

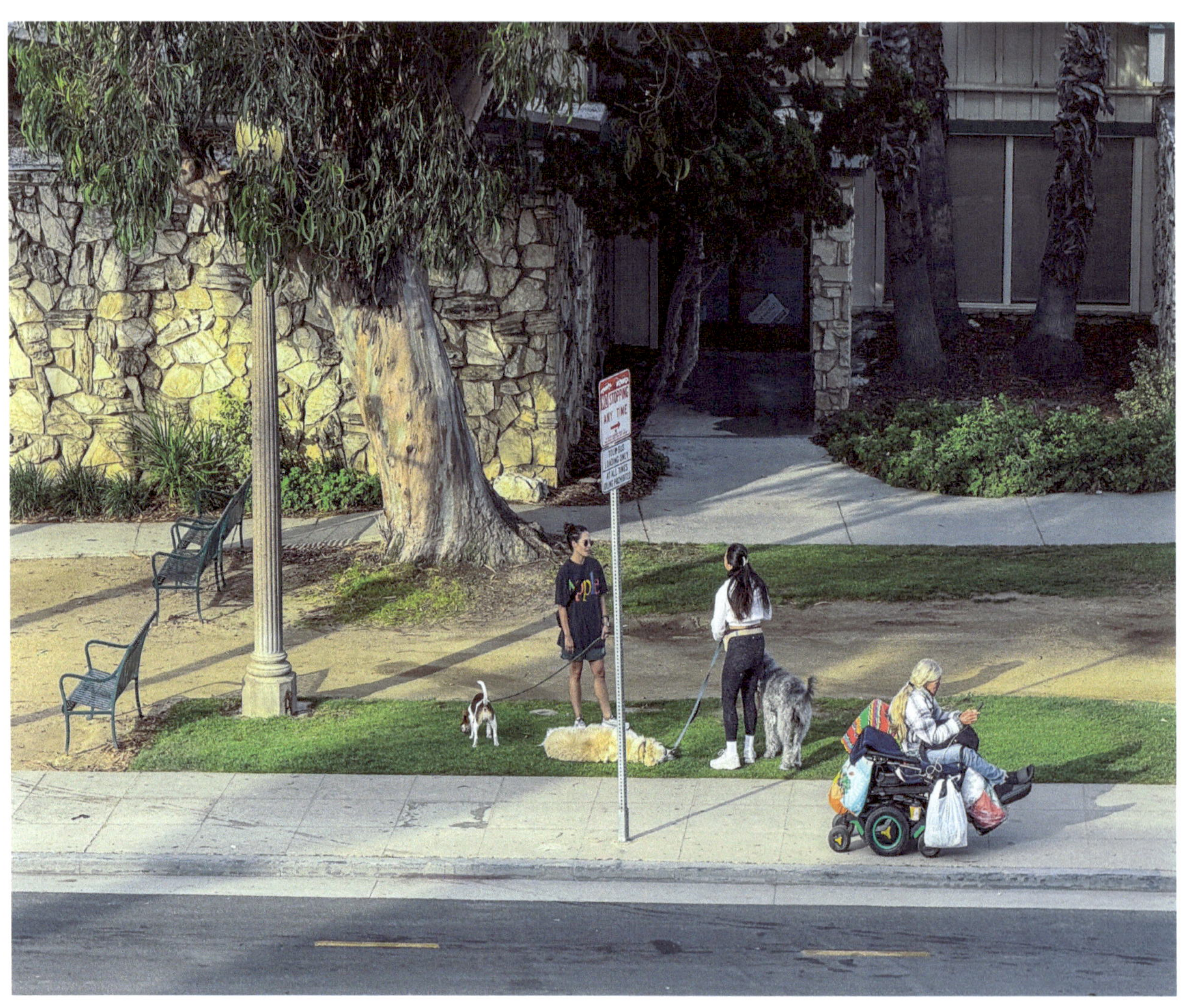

NO STOPPING
ANY TIME
TOUR BUS
LOADING ONLY
AT ALL TIMES
DOUBLE PARKING PROHIBITED

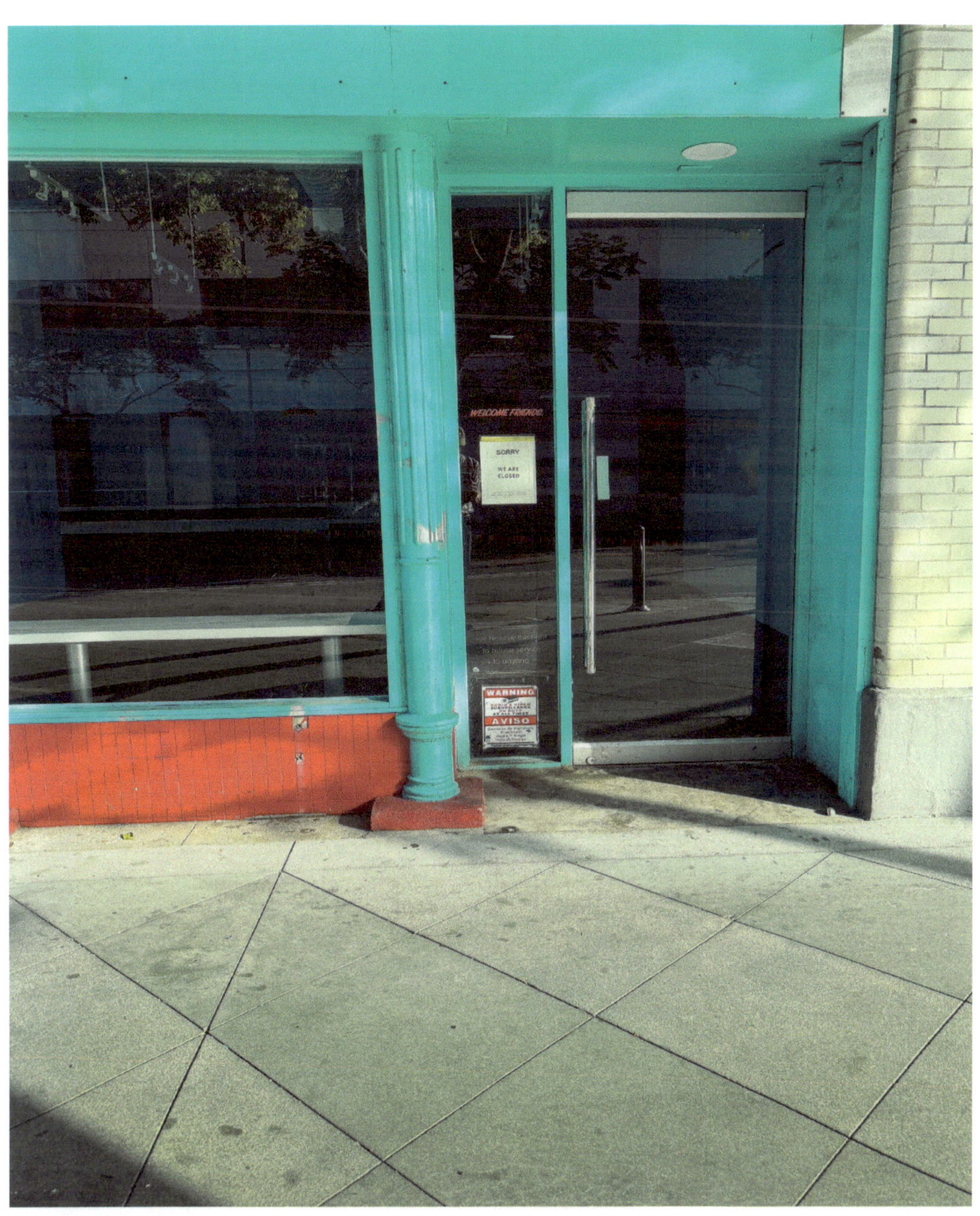
WELCOME FRIENDS.
SORRY
WE ARE
CLOSED
WARNING
AUDIO & VIDEO
SURVEILLANCE
IN DUTY
AT ALL TIMES
AVISO

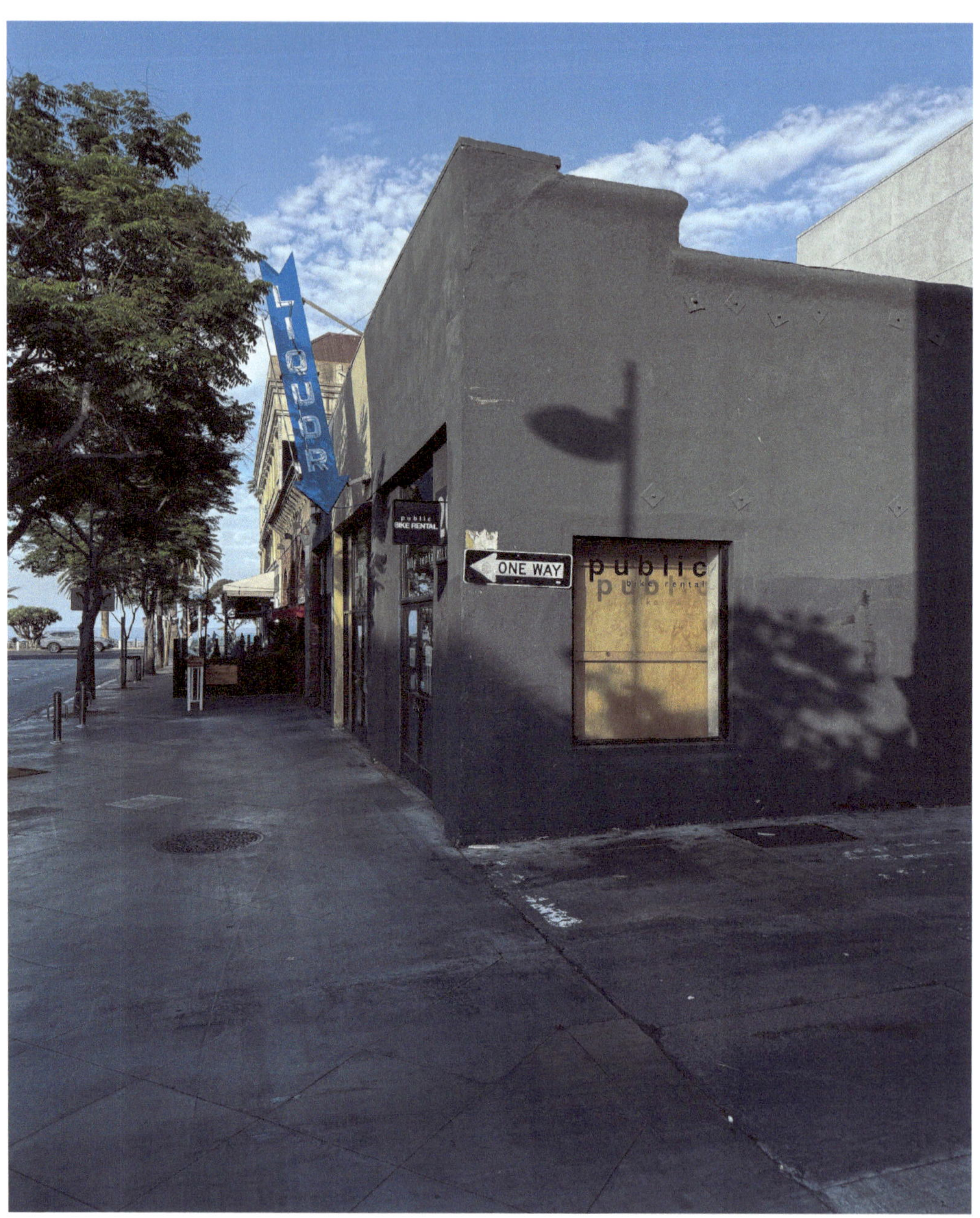

LIQUOR
public
BIKE RENTAL
ONE WAY
public

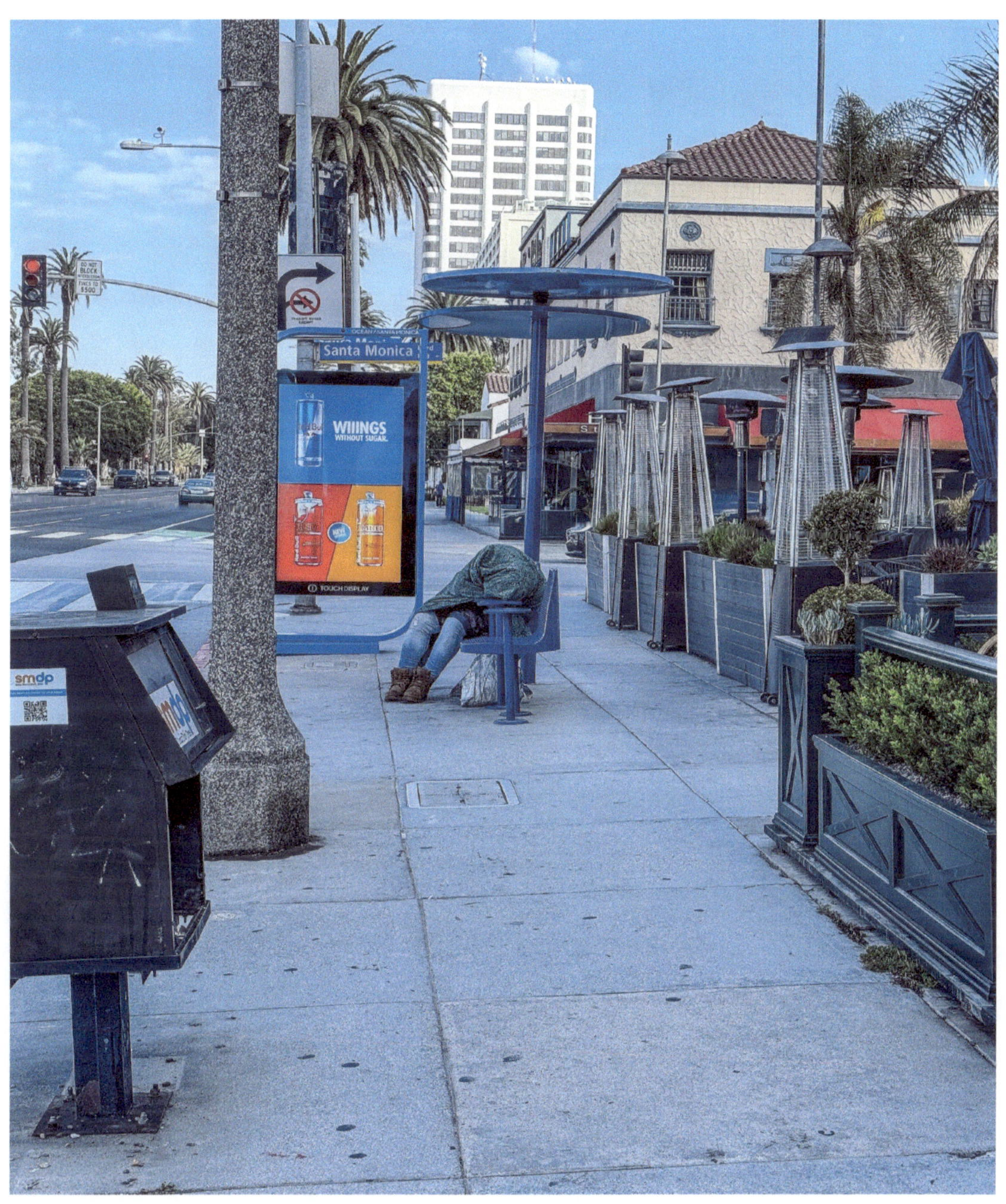

Santa Monica
WIIINGS
WITHOUT SUGAR
TOUCH DISPLAY
smdp
DO NOT BLOCK
FINES TO $500

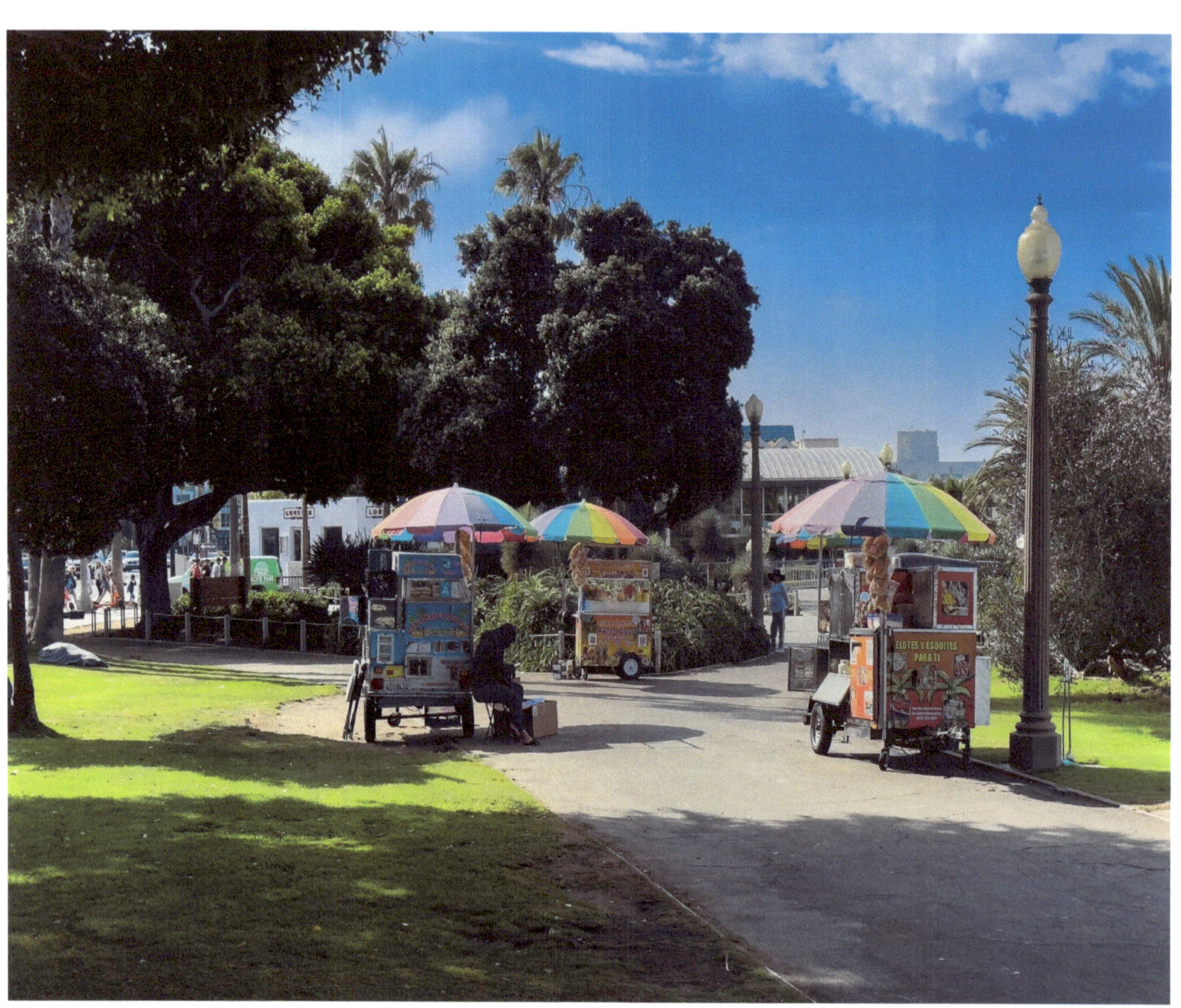

ELOTES Y ESQUITES
PARA TI

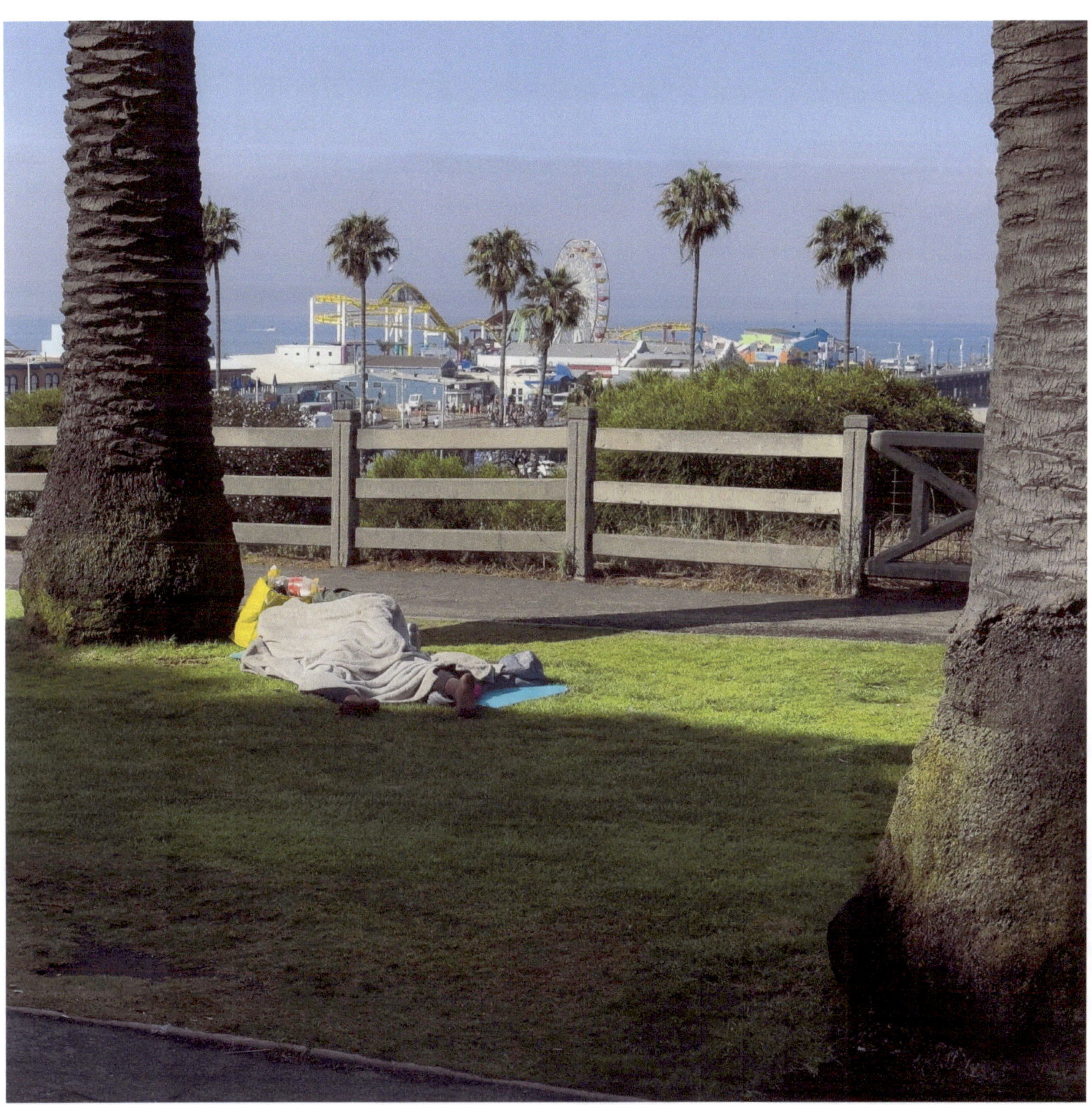

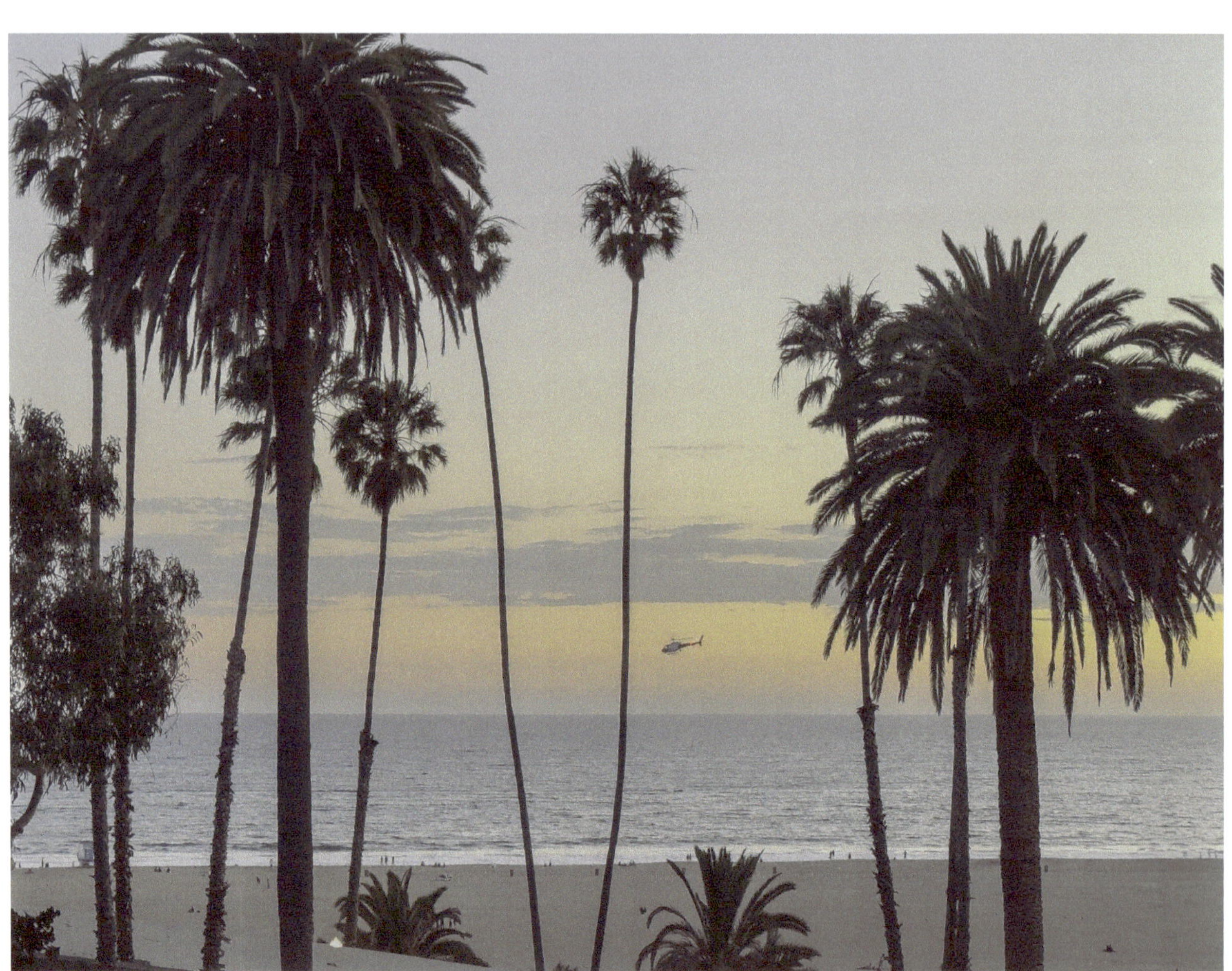

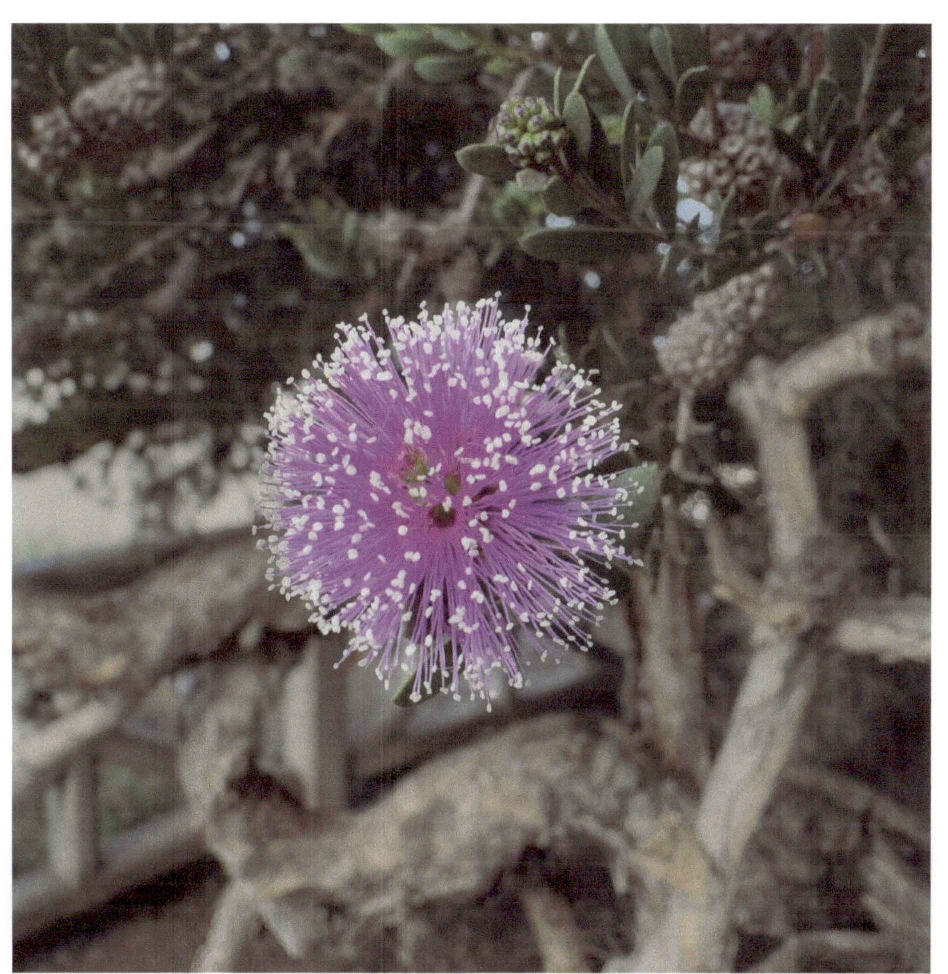

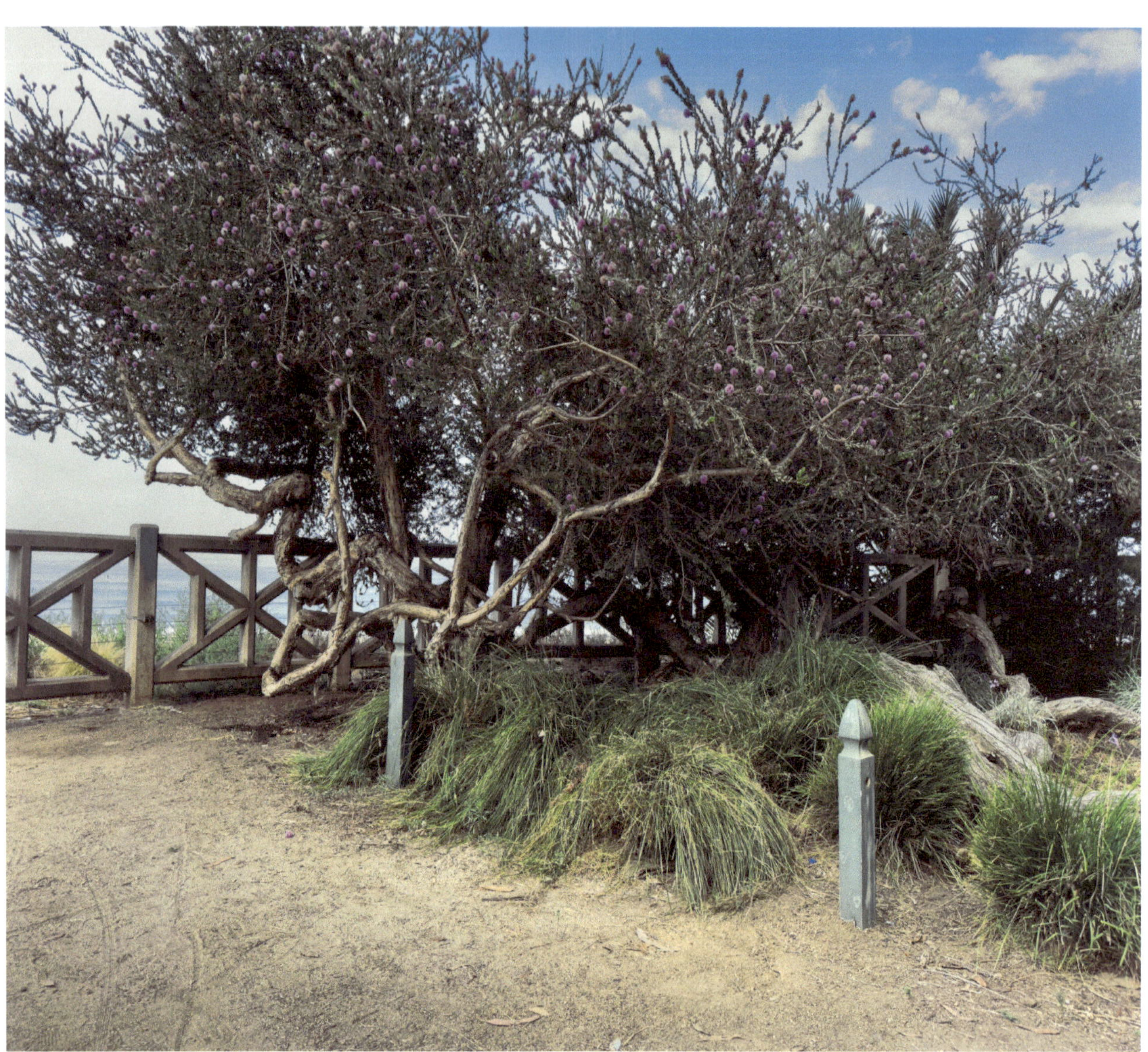

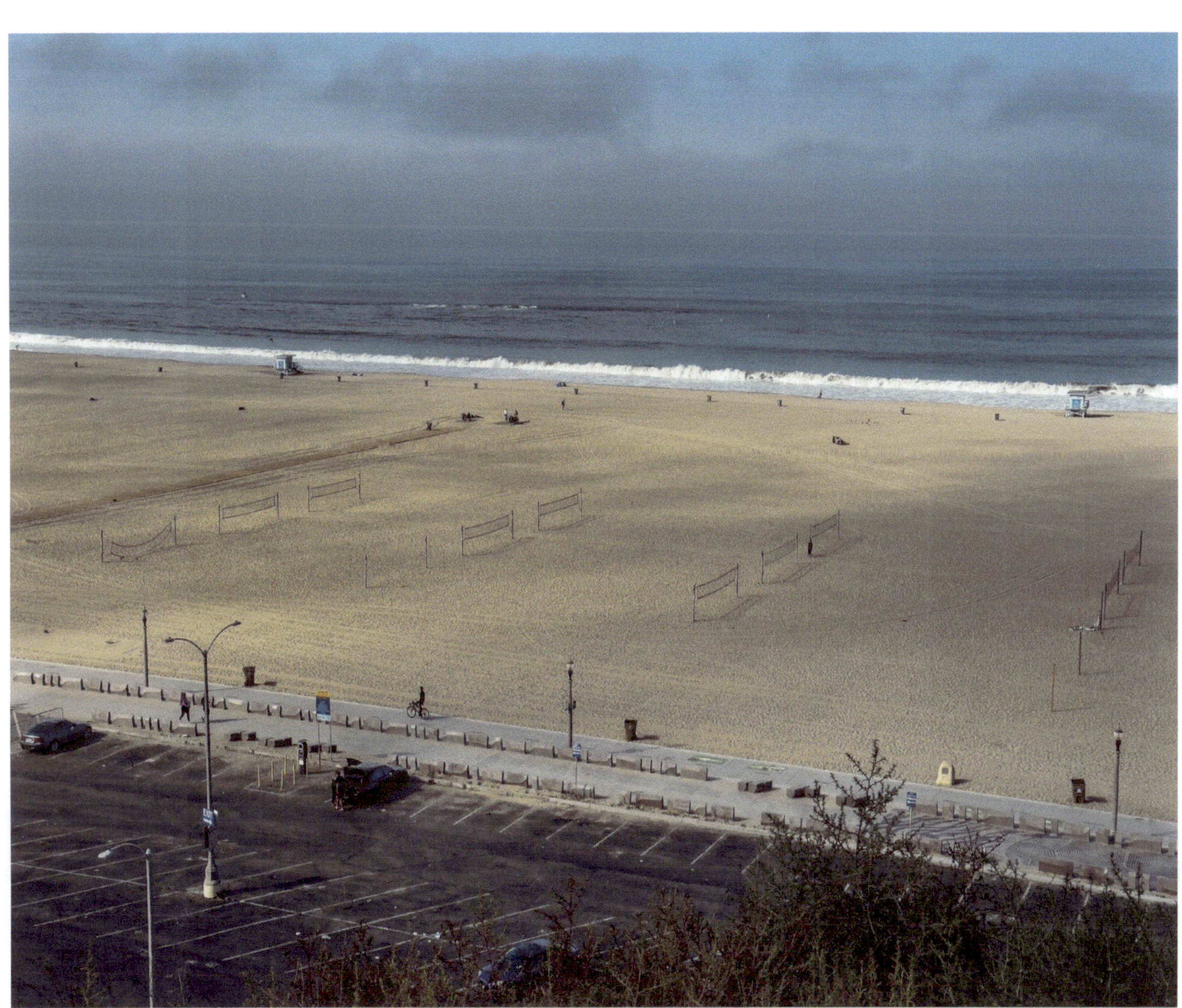

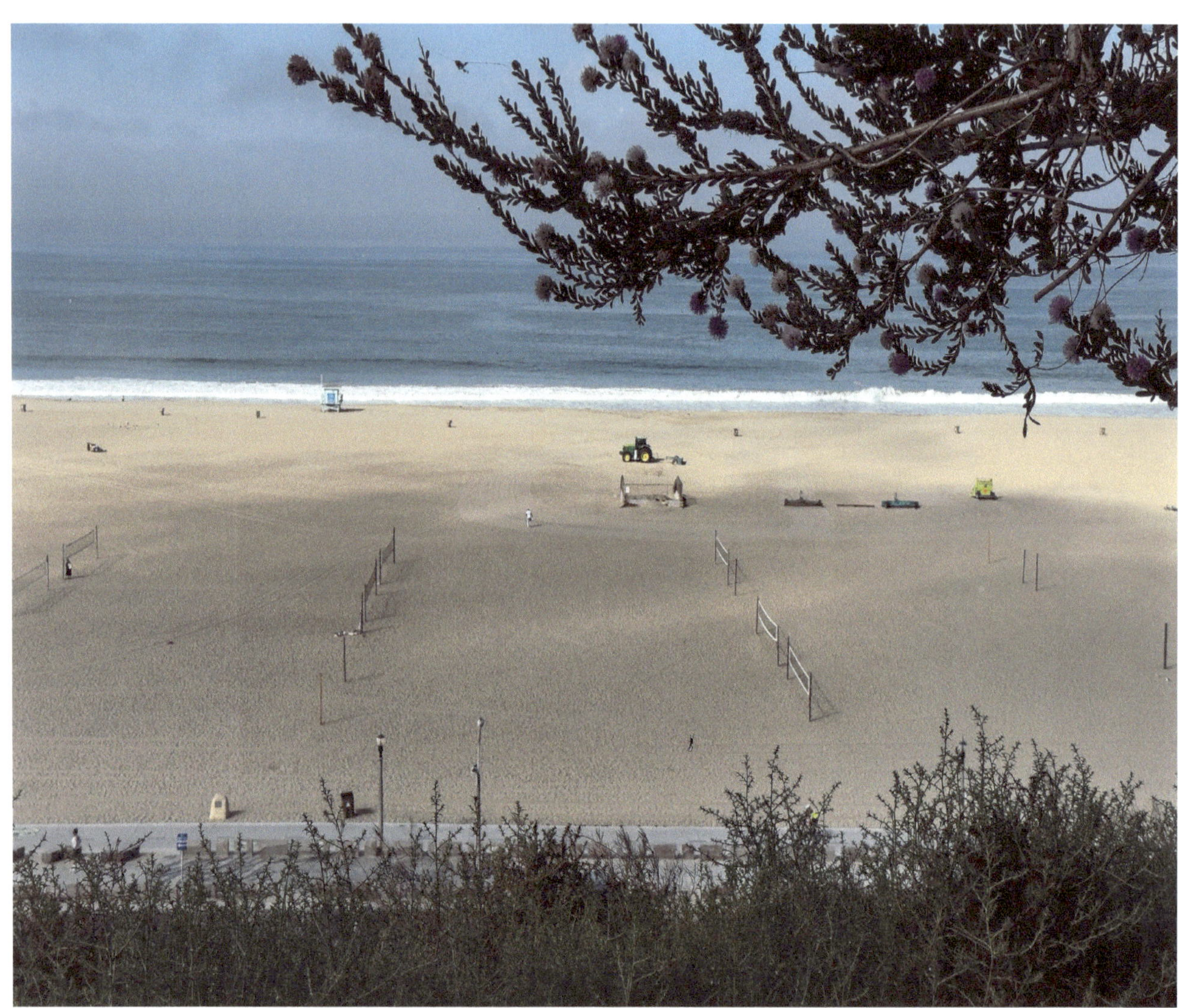

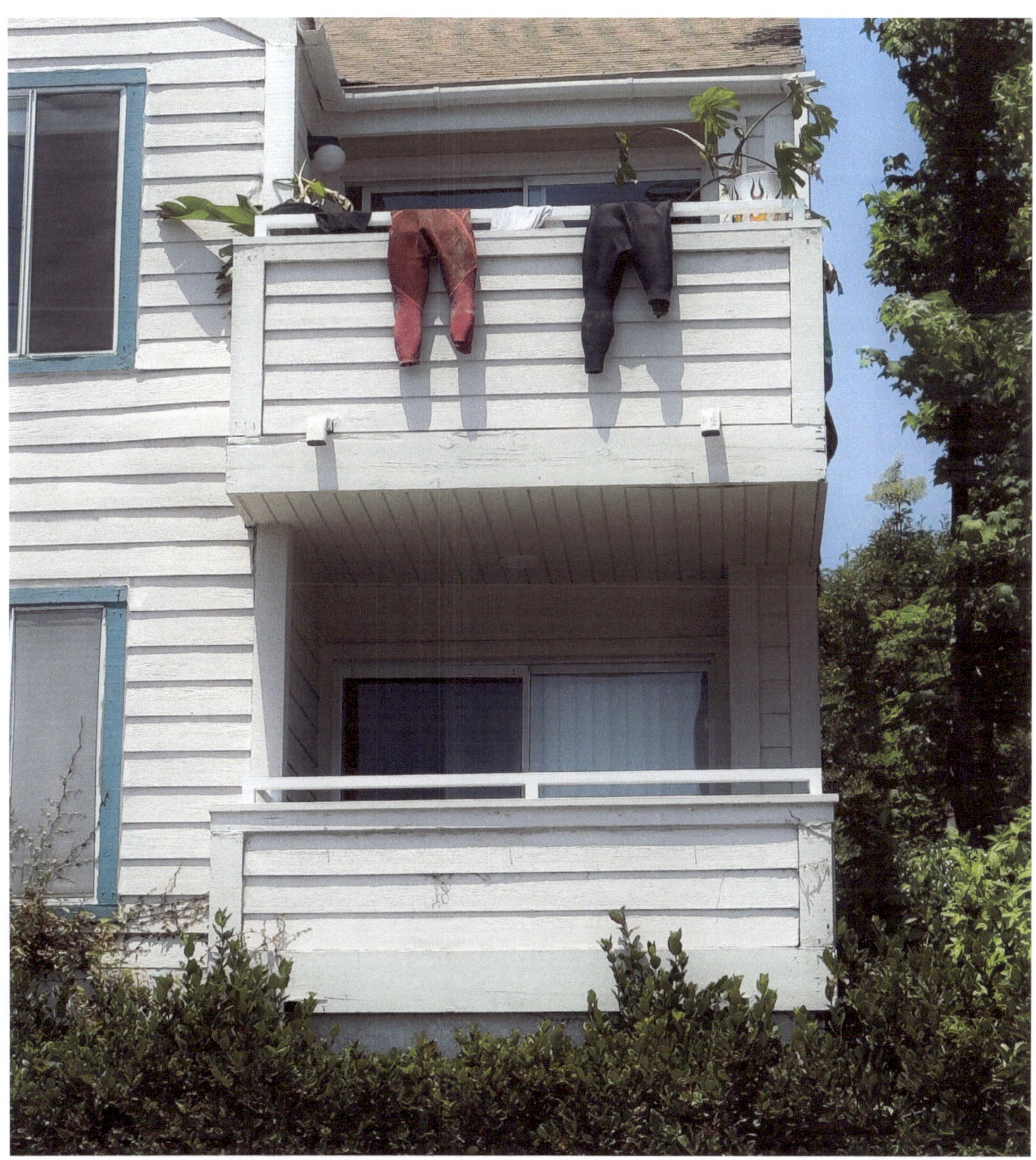

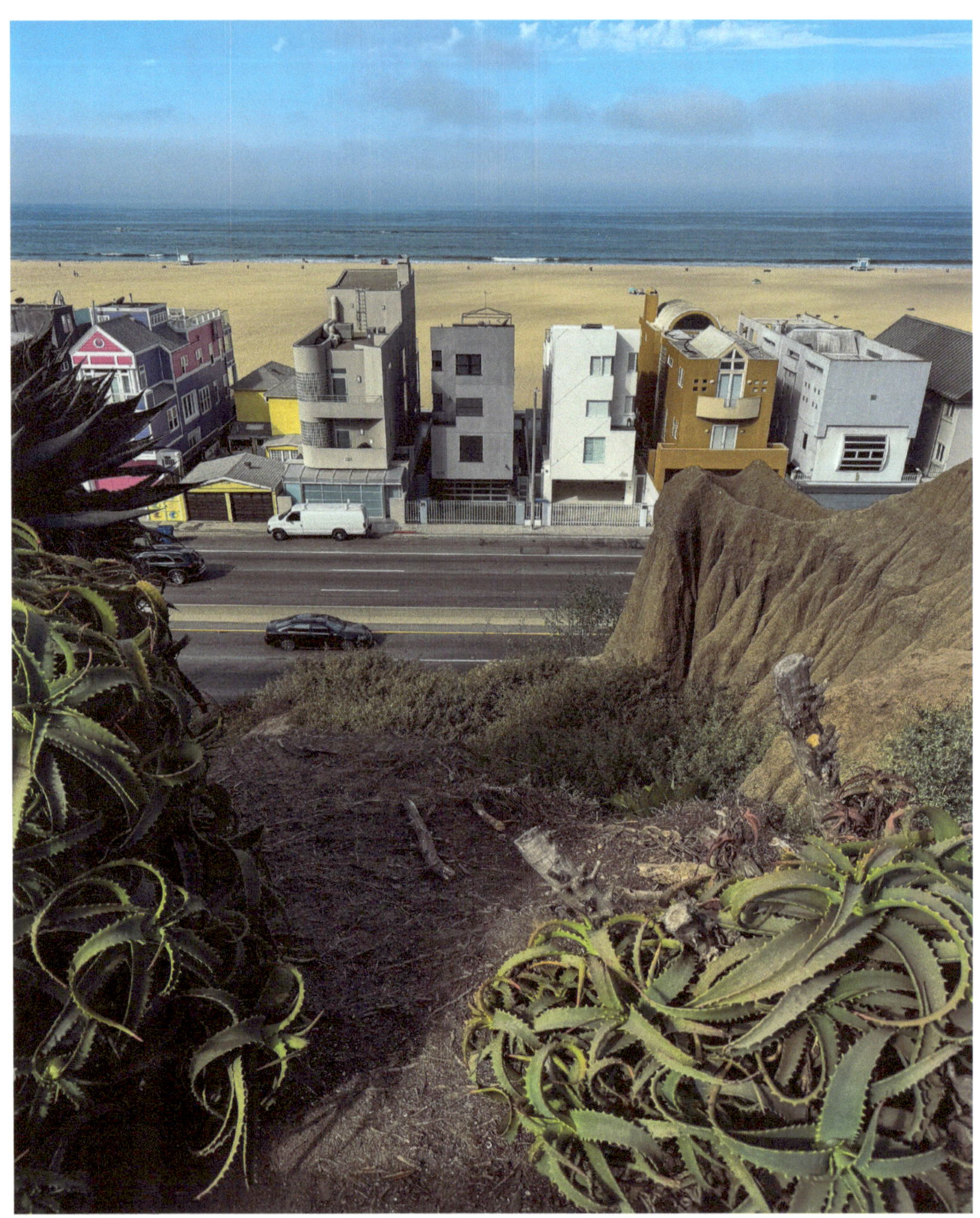

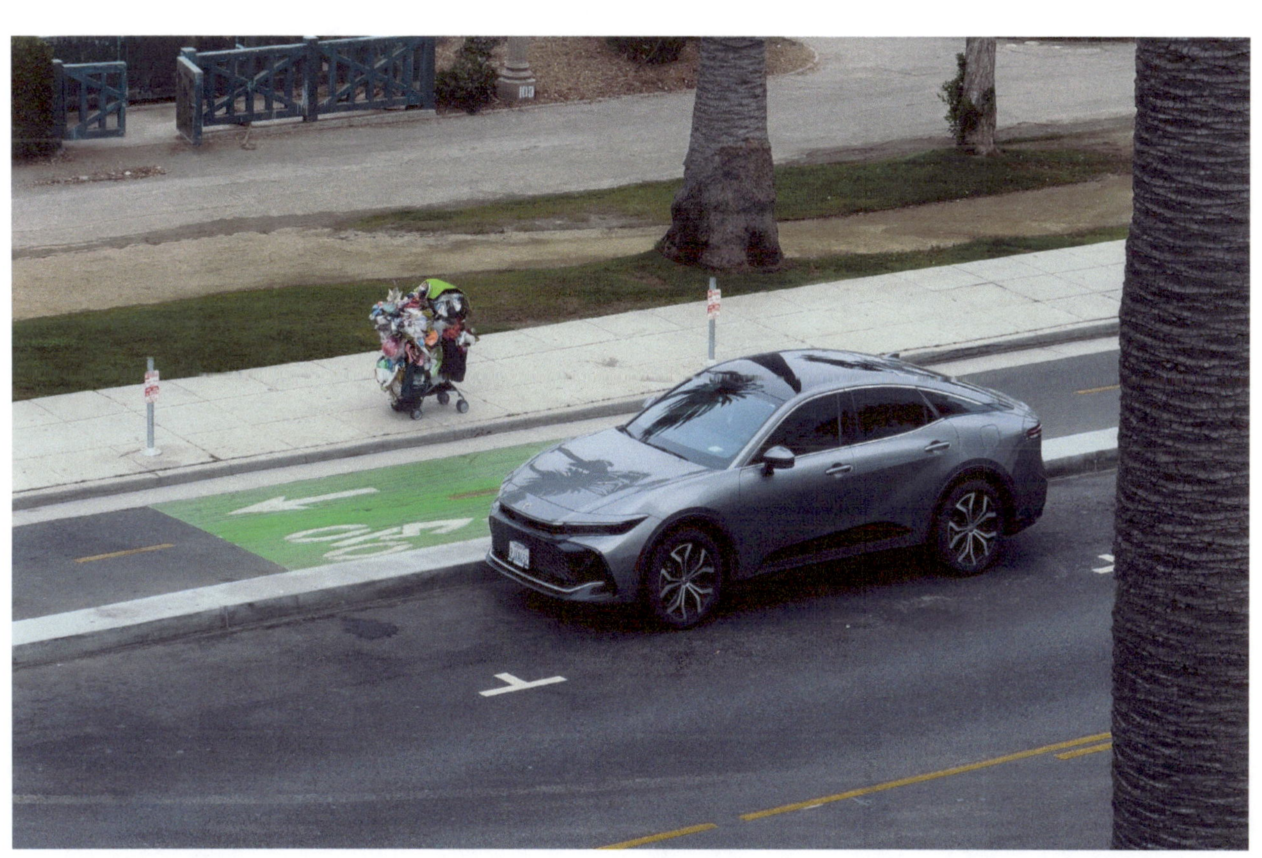

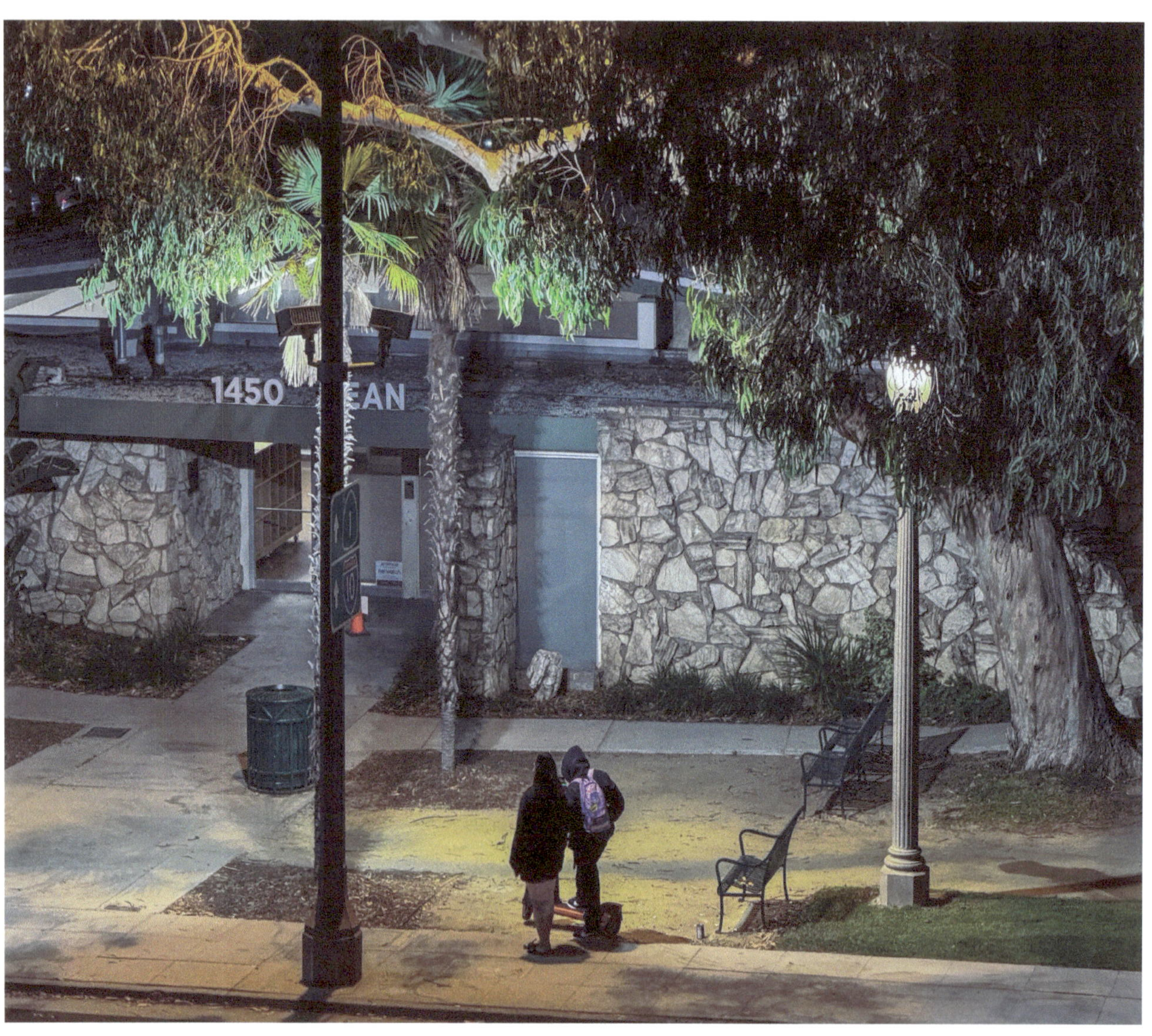

1450
EAN

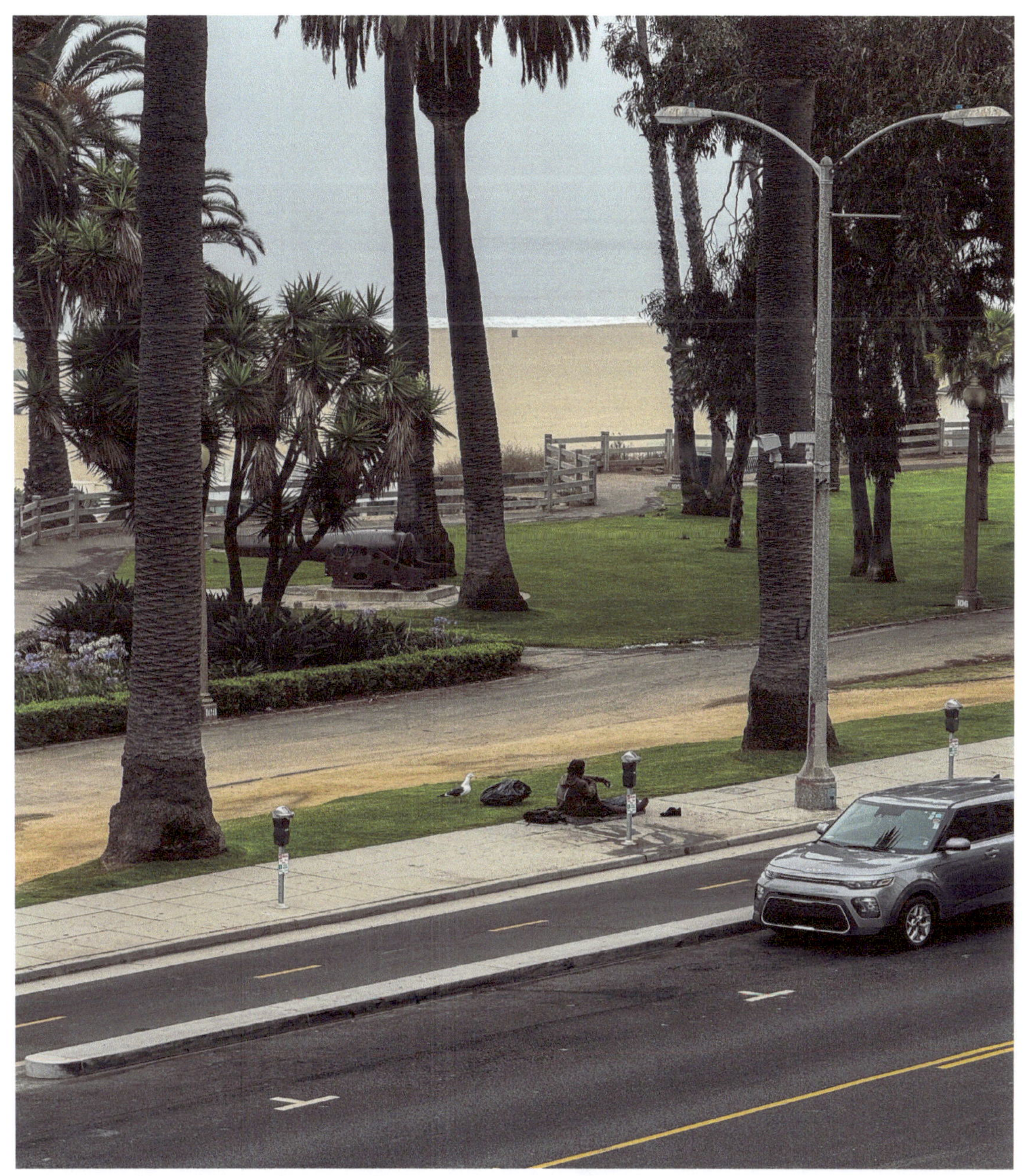

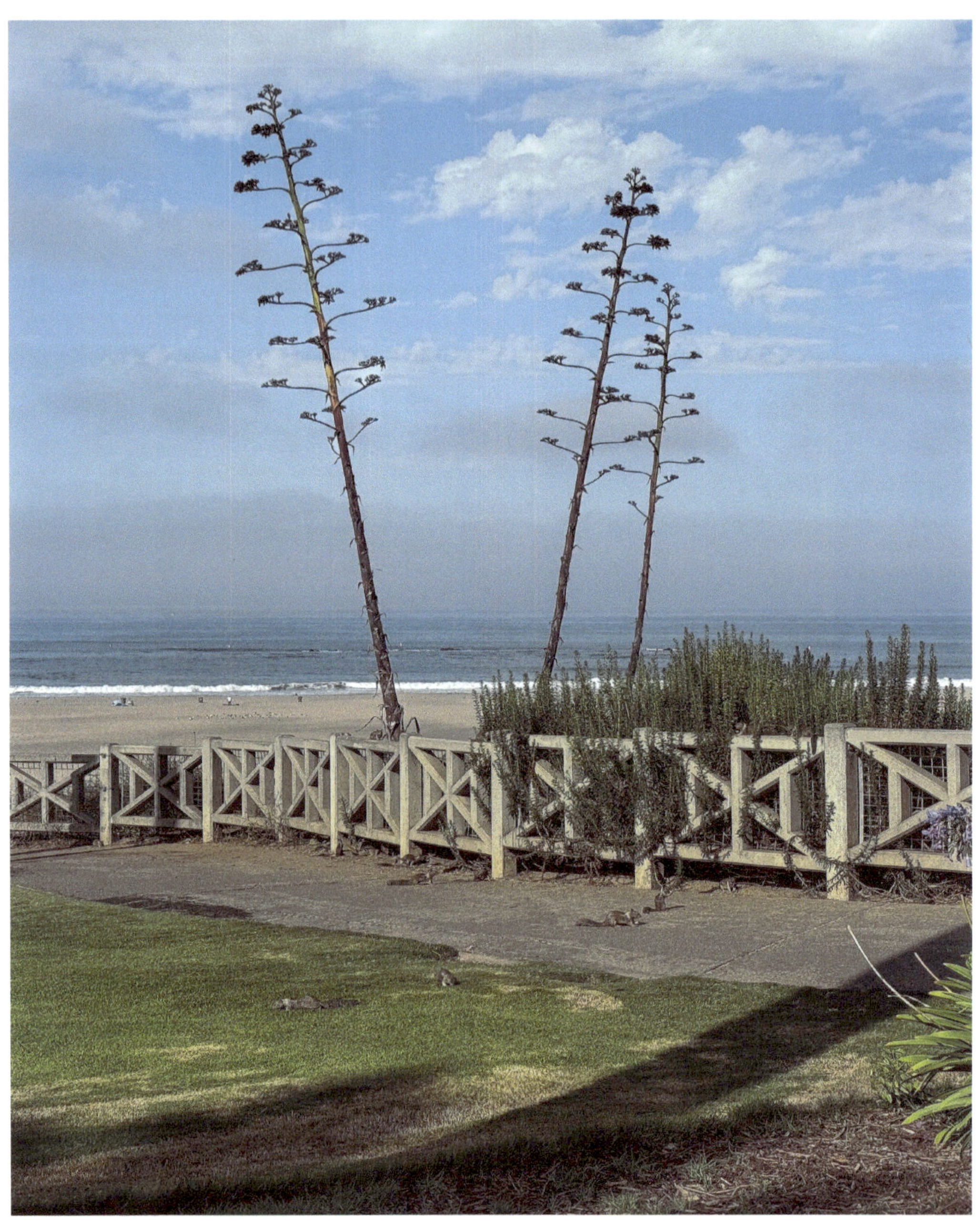

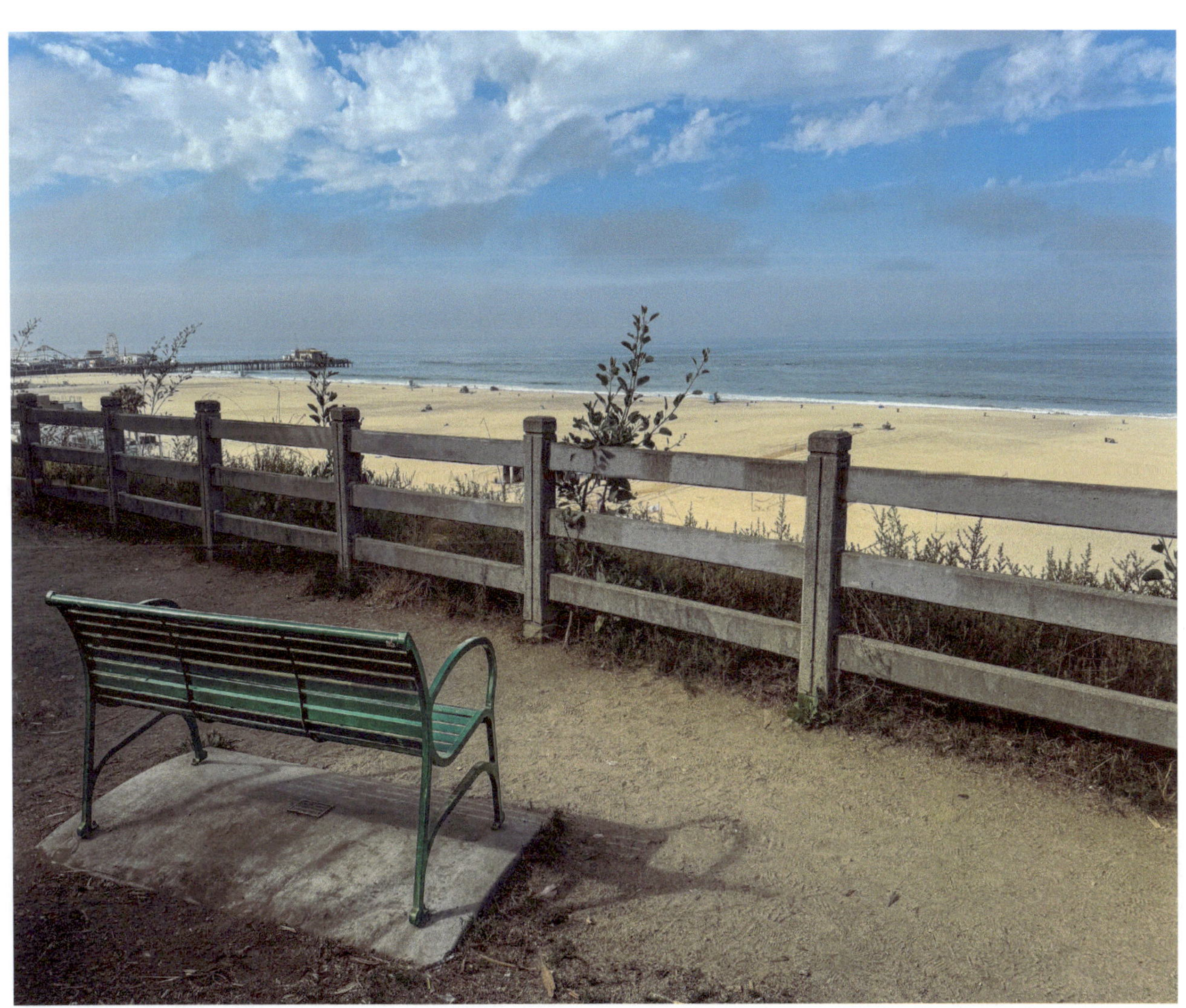

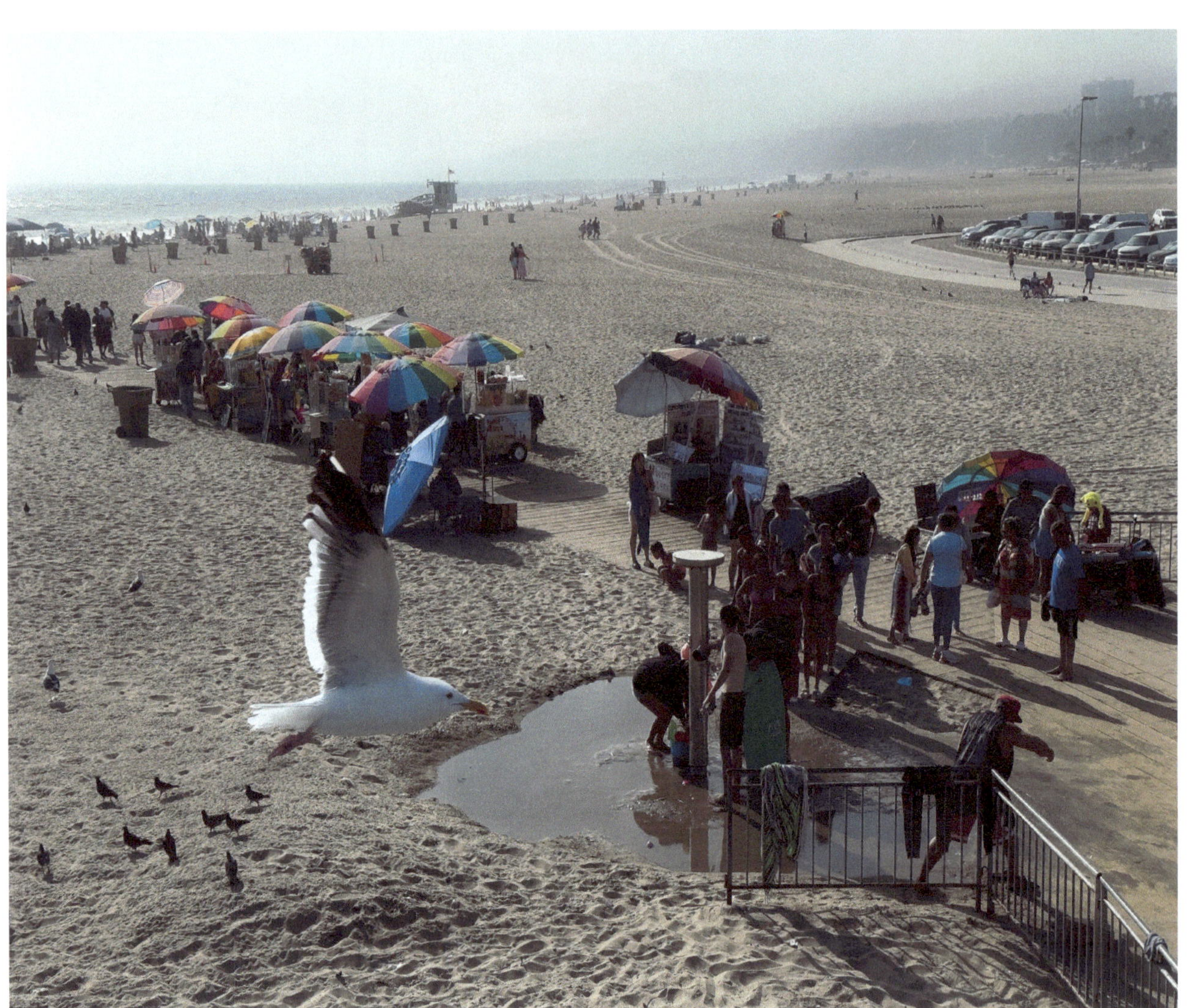

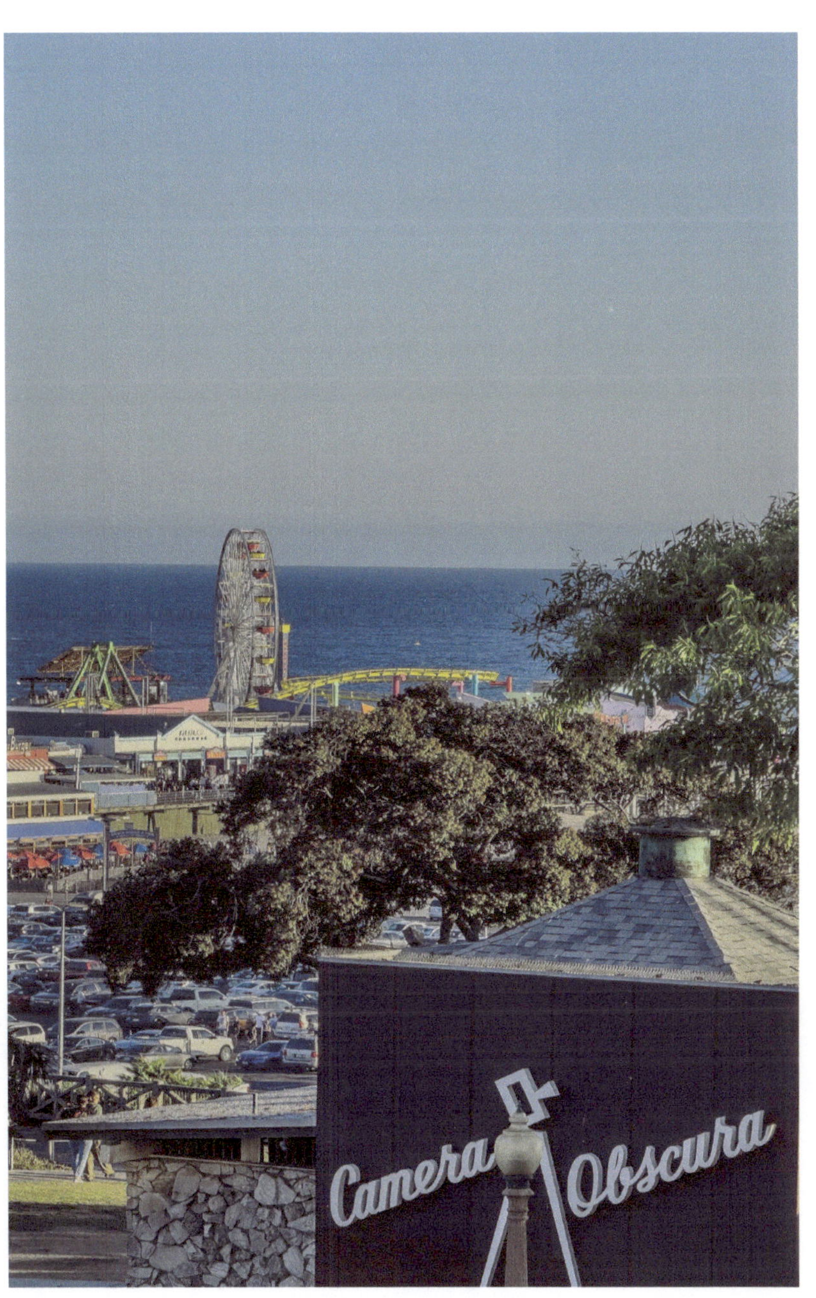
Camera
Obscura

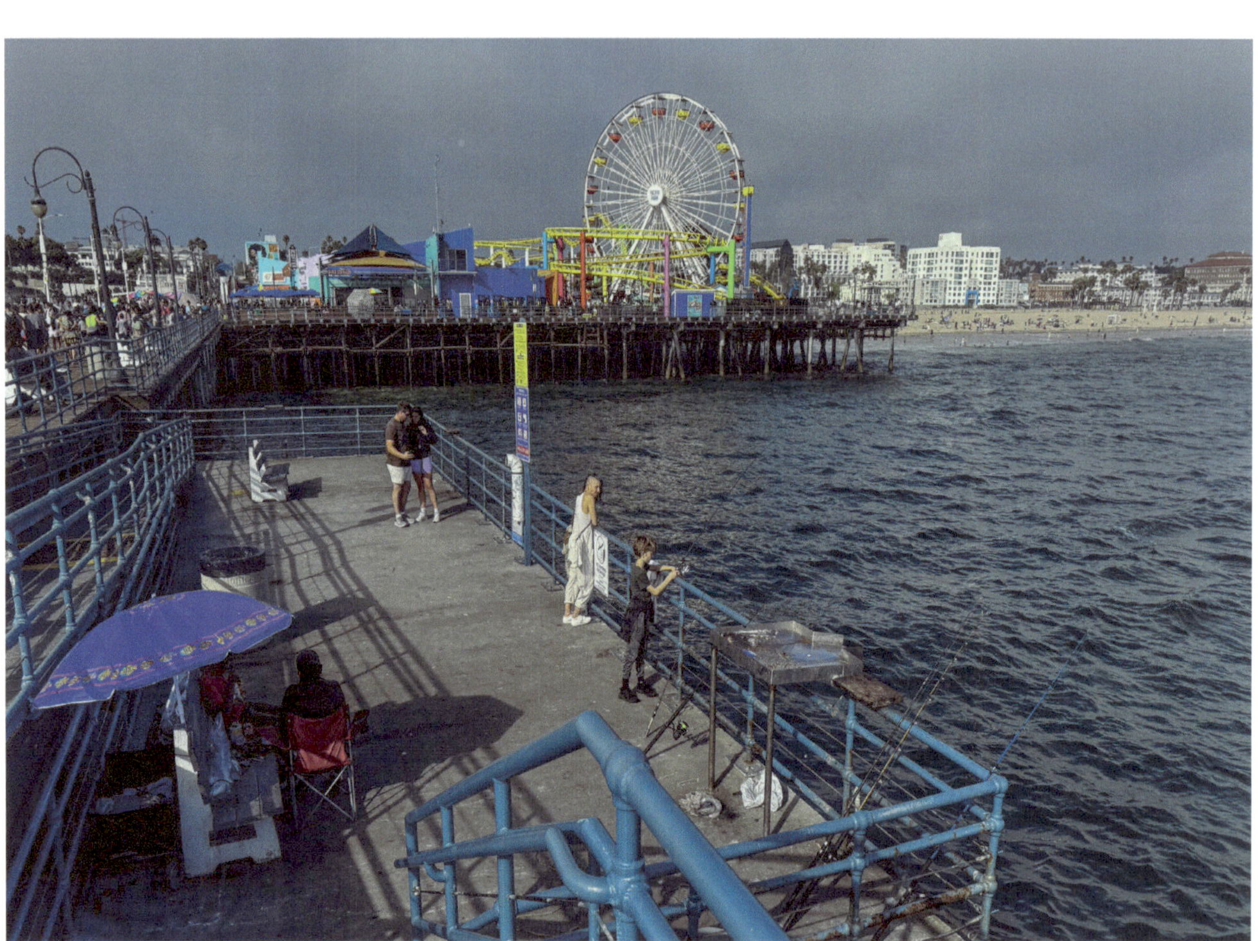

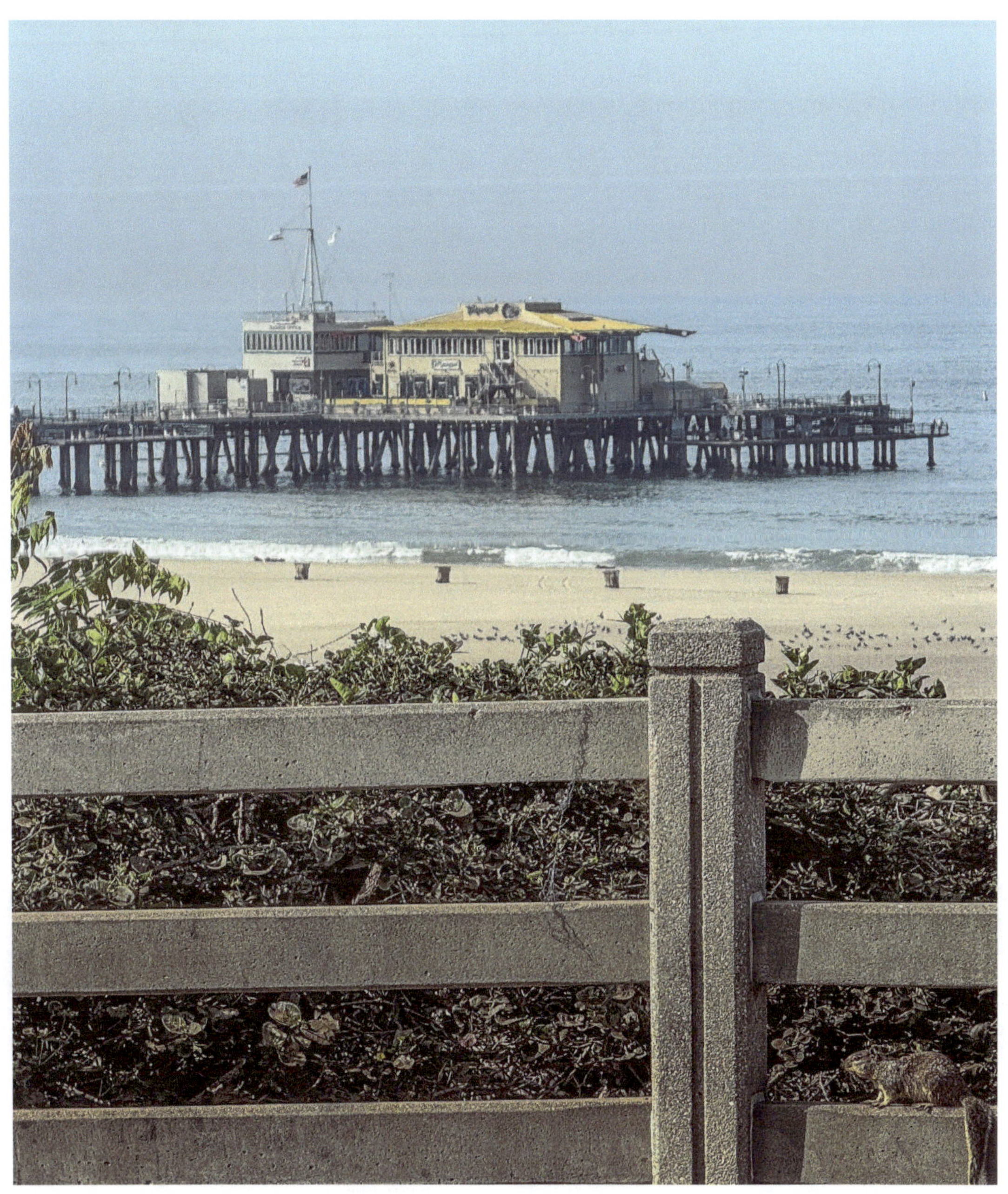

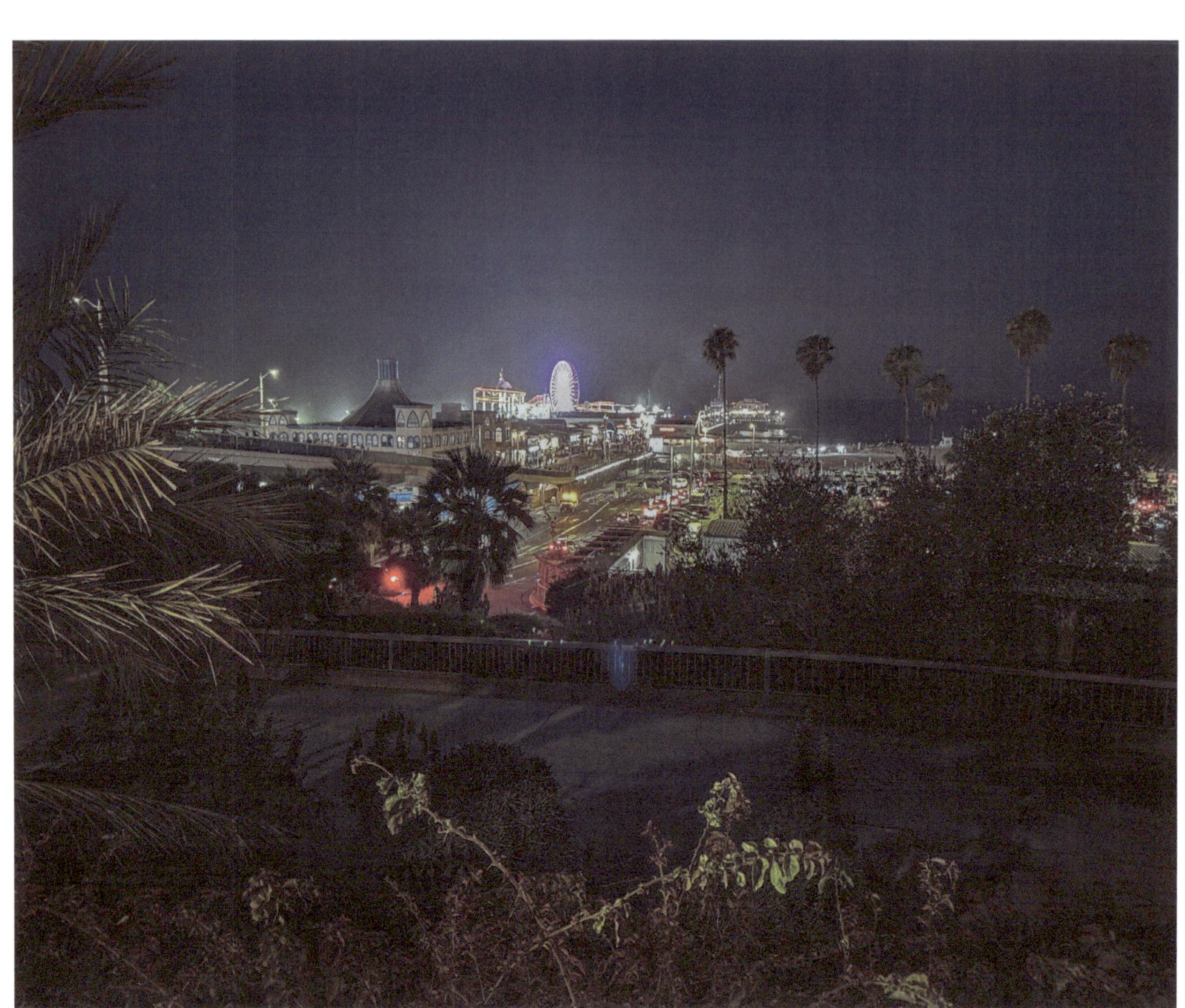

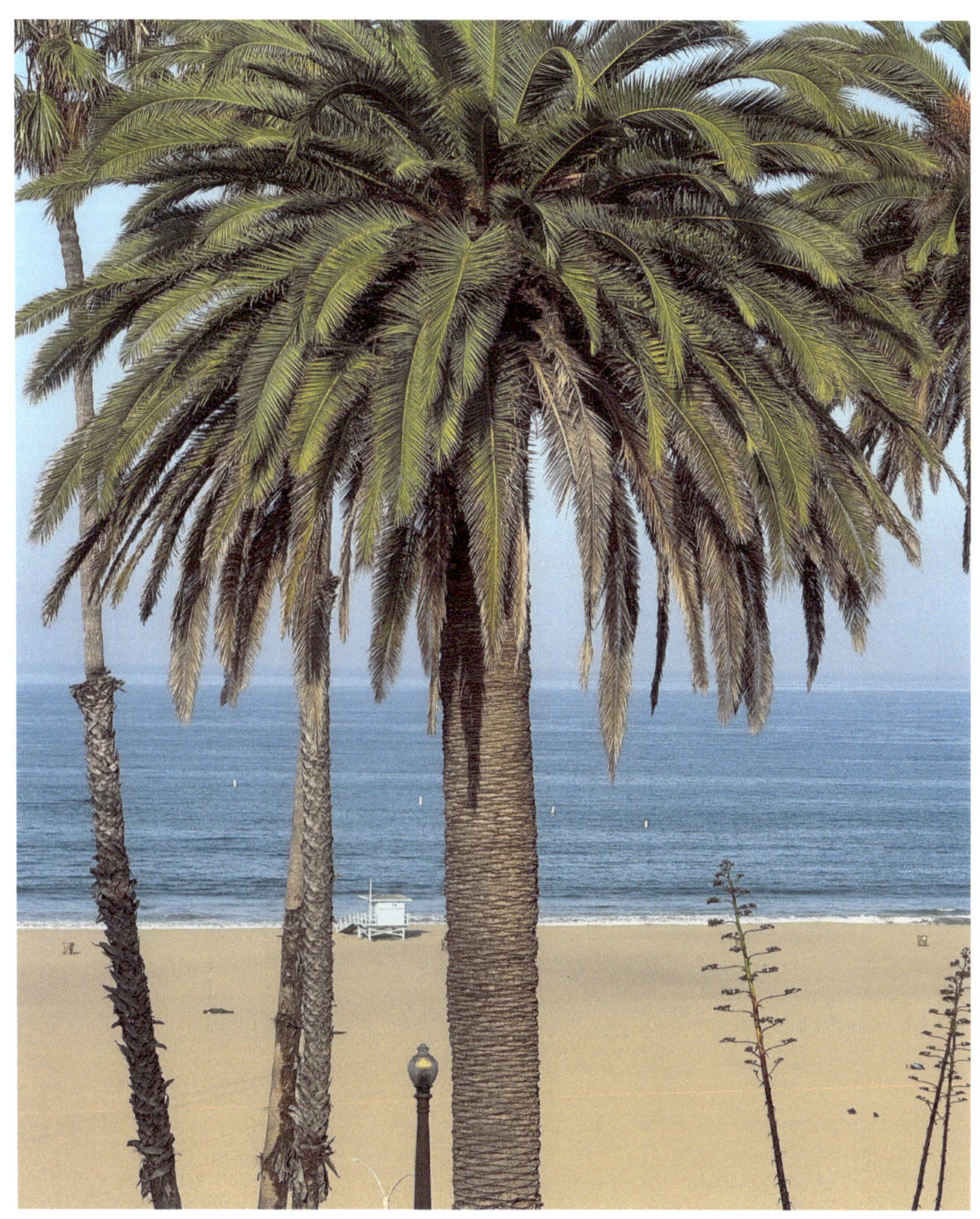

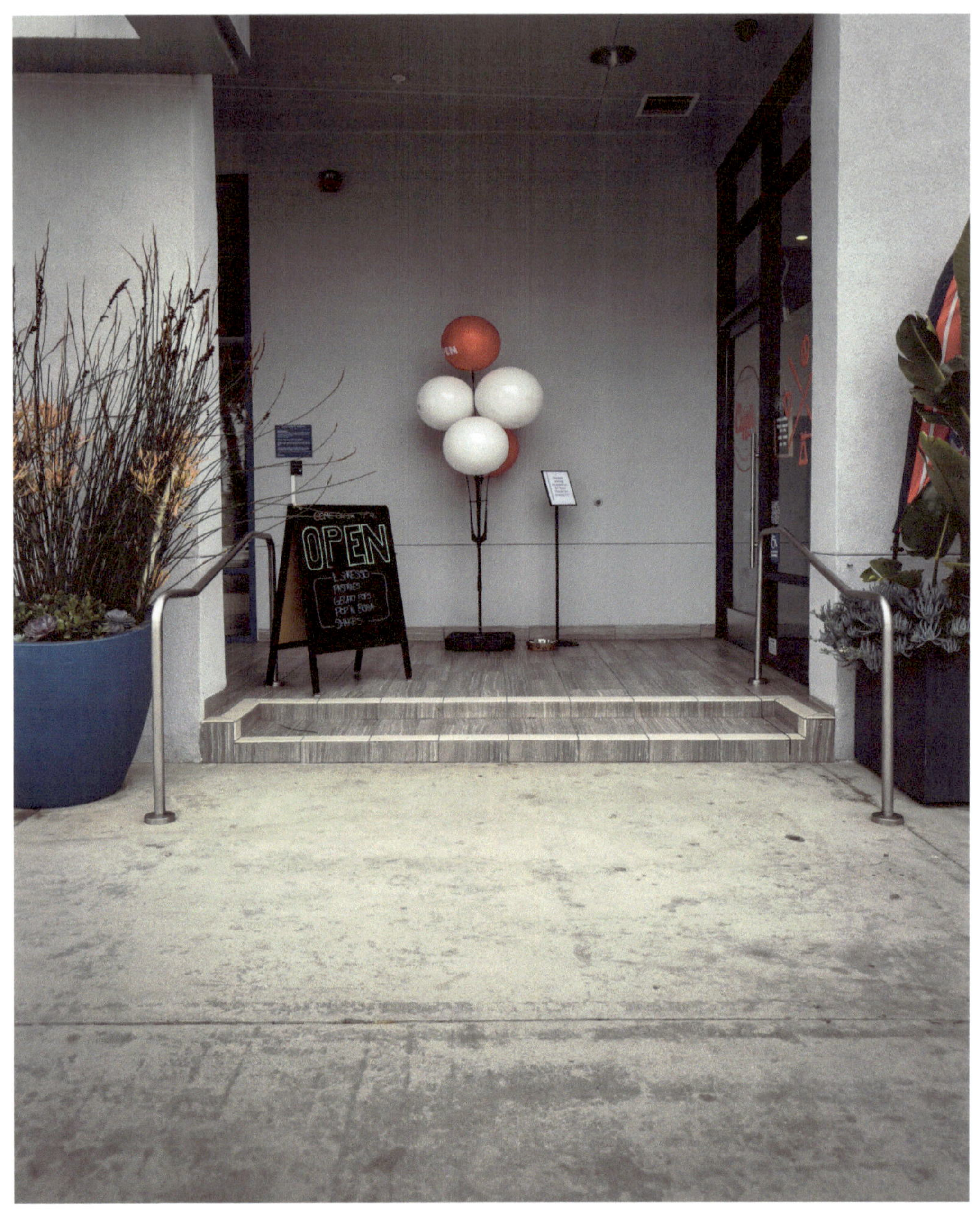

OPEN
ESPRESSO
PASTRIES
GELATO 95%
POP 'N SODA
SHAKES

REFLECTIONS

Speak your mind even though your voice shakes.

Eleanor Roosevelt

Homelessness is not a crime, but elitism should be.

www.ingramcontent.com/pod-product-compliance
Lightning Source LLC
Chambersburg PA
CBHW041949140726
48006CB00002BA/564